HIDDEN HISTORY
of
RAVENSWOOD
&
LAKE VIEW

Patrick Butler

Published by The History Press
Charleston, SC 29403
www.historypress.net

Copyright © 2013 by Patrick Butler
All rights reserved

Unless otherwise noted, all internal and cover images are from the Ravenswood–Lake View Historical Association collection.

First published 2013

Manufactured in the United States

ISBN 978.1.60949.867.2

Library of Congress CIP data applied for.

Notice: The information in this book is true and complete to the best of our knowledge. It is offered without guarantee on the part of the author or The History Press. The author and The History Press disclaim all liability in connection with the use of this book.

All rights reserved. No part of this book may be reproduced or transmitted in any form whatsoever without prior written permission from the publisher except in the case of brief quotations embodied in critical articles and reviews.

To Kathy Hills, without whose help and encouragement this book would not have been possible.

Contents

Acknowledgements 7
Introduction 9

Part I. Lake View
Waterfront Living at Its Best—and Strangest 13
Chicago Temple Chimes Still Honor Early Settler John Turner 16
John Peter Altgeld: Heroic Rags to Riches to Rags Story 18
North Side's Own "Valley of Kings" Was the "Living End" for Many 19
Lake View Joins Chicago—and Not Everyone Is Cheering 21
Samuel Gross's Business Included Eighteen Towns, Cyrano Novel 24
Streetcars, Trains Pulled It All Together on the Early North Side 27
When a Few Riverview Revelers Literally Died Laughing 31
Harms Park Was an Almost Nonstop Picnic for Fifty-four Years 34
Ultimate "Party Animal" Charlie Weber Left Plenty of Questions 36
Guardsmen Went After Pancho Villa as Practice for Great War 37
First World War's Front Lines Ran Down "Lincolnstrasse" 39
Armistice Sent Neighbors Pouring into Streets to Celebrate, Fight 41
Twenties Roared through Lake View Despite Prohibition, Recession 42
Lake View Marked Fiftieth as War Again Broke Out in Europe 44
Local Germans Took the Lead in Wartime Bond Drives 44
Hitler Kin Sounded Warning about Uncle during Visit to Temple 46
North Side's Own "Benedict Arnold" Didn't Get Away with It 47
Enola Gay's Bomb Bays Blew Cover Off Local Soldier's Secret 49
V-J Day Brought Cheers, Tears on Lake View Streets 50
For Some, D-Day Reenactment Fifty Years Later Was Far Too Real 51
When de Valera Won One for Irish Freedom at Wrigley Field 52
March 17, 1948: The Night the Music, and Anne Hunt, Died 54
Lake View High's Teachers Wrote Their Own Legends, Their Way 55

Contents

Lane Tech, Like Its Namesake, Was a Mix of Brains and Brawn	56
Olympic Legend Avery Brundage Made a Lasting Mark Here	58
1896 "Great Race" Wasn't Much to Write Home About	59
"Where's the Beef?" Cops Wondered in Spring of 1897	61
Arabs, Jews Still Pray for This Christian Couple a Century Later	62
Rube Goldberg Would Have Loved These Guys Back in the Day	64
Cop Shop, Ballpark, CHA Homes, Theater Prove Reincarnation	65
1971 Indian "Uprising" Spreads from Ballpark to Missile Site	71
Archbishop Sheil Got Boys Boxing, Battled Bigotry and Fear	72
Early North Side Park Was Literally Scooped Out of Clay…	73
…and Clay Made Lake View Center of U.S. Terra Cotta Industry	74
Why Some Carpenters, Stable Owners Saw Future in Next World	75
"Yellow Kid" Weil Wished He'd Gone into Politics Instead of Jail	77
Swedish Roots Still Run Deep Enough for Two Visits by King	78
"Children's Poet" Eugene Field Gone but Never Forgotten	81

Part II. Ravenswood

Is Ravenswood a State of Mind or a Real Neighborhood?	83
Unsung Civil War Hero May Have Helped Save Chicago	89
For Last Trooper, Living Poor Here Was Worse than Indian Wars	90
North Center Was Once Just That—the Center of the North Side	91
Back in the Day, Ravenswood—not LA—Was for Star-Gazing	93
Faith Can Move Mountains—and Even Our Lady of Lourdes	94
Abe Saperstein Began His Globetrotting Career at Welles Park	96
Famed Architect Louis Sullivan Wrapped Up His Career Here	97
Abbott's First Lab Was Run Out of Town by Irate Neighbors	98
47th Ward Was Scene of a Generation-Long "Duel of the Titans"	101
"Inebriated, Opium-Eating Women" Helped at Washington Clinic	104
Sweet Smell of Success Lingers On at Buffalo, Horner Parks	106
Channel Helped Clean Up after "Epidemic" that Never Happened	109
Three Brothers Who Became Admirals Got Their Start Here	111
Army's Top Engineer Spent Decades Trying to Prove Innocence	112
Forgotten Musical Star's Legacy Still Lives On at Local Library	113
Keeping Kids in School Was a Lifelong Battle for William Bodine	114
Curt Teich Brought the World Home with 265,000 Postcards	116
North Center Radio Pioneer Tuned Out, Bet on Local Paper	117
"Hero" Turned Out to Be the Killer in Sensational Mystery Here	118
Memories of Temperance Groups, Local Militias Still on Display	119
Ravenswood Women's Club Was as Victorian as It Could Get	121
Was Bowmanville Named for Innkeeper Who Swindled Guests?	122
Ravenswood Residents Played Own Version of "Name Game"	125

Bibliography	127
About the Author	128

Acknowledgements

Many thanks to:

Julie Lynch, archivist at the Sulzer Regional Library, for her tireless assistance;

Former Sulzer Regional Library director Leah Steele for her guidance and encouragement;

The Ravenswood–Lake View Historical Association;

The Chicago History Museum Library;

My daughter Kathleen Butler Greenan, son-in-law Ryan Greenan and Chicago author Richard Lindberg for their support, each in their own inimitable ways; and to F. Bryan Pickett for technical support.

And The History Press, especially Ben Gibson, my commissioning editor, for making this happen.

INTRODUCTION

Chicago's Lake View/Ravenswood area might just be the only place in America where you would have found a Civil War prisoner of war camp, the world's first Ferris wheel, Nazi rallies in what was then promoted as the world's largest amusement park and a "cursed" totem pole near the lakefront that has supposedly kept the Chicago Cubs from winning the World Series.

This *Hidden History of Ravenswood and Lake View* was never intended to be your average history book so much as a kind of curio shop of people and places that time forgot. You probably didn't know, for example, that the first long-distance phone call from suburban Ravenswood to Chicago was made from John Hill's tavern at Clark and Leland in 1870; that some of the first cowboy movies—featuring stars like Tom Mix—were made at Selig Studios at 1815 West Larchmont; that Lincoln Avenue was once a toll road from Irving Park to Berwyn; or that in 1883, horse-drawn "omnibuses" took Ravenswood residents from a livery stable at Lawrence and Ravenswood to vote at city hall. By 1874, in fact, Ravenswood was being touted as one of Chicagoland's best suburbs.

Over the next 125 pages or so, we'll cheer American-born Irish revolutionary (and future Irish president) Eamon DeValera at a floodlit Wrigley Field nighttime rally where none of the neighbors voiced any complaints about lights in an era when illuminated ballparks were unheard of. We'll meet a buttoned-up Ravenswood land developer who may have helped end the Civil War at least a year earlier by thwarting a plan to free

Introduction

several thousand Confederates from a South Side prison so they could launch a surprise attack behind Union army lines. And we'll marvel at the chutzpah of Lake View mayor Billy Boldenweck, who refused to hand over the then-suburb's records and funds after its 1889 annexation by Chicago.

Fueled by a steady stream of refugees from the 1871 Chicago Fire, Lake View has grown from nineteenth-century German blue collar to 1960s hippie to contemporary yuppie, all the while retaining icons like Wrigley Field, now the nation's second-oldest major-league ballpark, built on the site of a long-forgotten Lutheran seminary; and the town hall police station, built in 1907 on the site of the former Lake View City Hall where Boldenweck briefly resisted a virtual siege after his constituents voted to become part of Chicago.

German and Swedish immigration triggered a major building boom between the mid-1880s and the onset of World War I. Because both groups—made up largely of building tradesmen who knew the difference—demanded well-built housing, a lot of those earlier buildings still survive.

By the early 1970s, one local commentator was writing about the "Layer Cake of Lake View," made up of low-income Hispanics to the west, German immigrants and their children in the middle and an influx of young professionals along the lakefront in what was then called "New Town."

Lake View was also fast becoming an incubator for independent politics in a Democratic "machine" stronghold dominated by the elder mayor Richard Daley—"The Real Mayor Daley," as far as some old-timers are concerned. As they had been doing for at least a century, Democratic ward committeemen and their precinct captains dispensed jobs and other favors to the party faithful who diligently brought in landslide votes for the "organization" and its candidates. But the "lakefront liberals'" day was coming fast in the wake of the Shakman Decree effectively outlawing most forms of political hiring and promotions.

It was not only an age of political reform along much of the North Side lakefront but also the heyday of community groups like the Lake View Citizens Council, born in 1952 to crack down on "bad bars" on Broadway and Clark Street; by the 1980s, it stopped the "machine" dead in its tracks when it tried to fill an aldermanic vacancy with someone who didn't even live in the ward. "We didn't realize we were coming up against the best organized community in Chicago," a somewhat chagrined city hall operative confided a few years later.

By the mid-1960s, Latinos (Puerto Ricans and some Mexicans) were pouring into the area, attracted by cheap rents and plentiful entry-level jobs.

Introduction

They were soon displaced by a yuppie invasion with its attendant pricey restaurants, fern bars and condos.

Just to the north, the Ravenswood community's boundaries depended on whether you asked the city, the Ravenswood Community Council or the now-defunct Ravenswood Chamber of Commerce. Although Ravenswood also attracted Chicago's well-to-do fleeing the fire and the all-too-common cholera and typhoid epidemics, one of the community's first businesses was the Sunnyside Inn at Clark and Montrose, a popular roadhouse once best known for its ethically flexible ladies. Another tavern, the even more notorious Shadyside Inn, went up across the street.

But no matter where you draw its boundaries, Ravenswood probably got its biggest shot in the arm with the help of a commuter railroad and what is now the Chicago transit system's Brown Line, now the busiest elevated route in the entire rapid transit network. It's hard to believe that only thirty years ago, the Chicago Transit Authority was seriously thinking of tearing down the Brown Line's tracks because it didn't expect to see enough future ridership to sustain the daily cost of service, let alone future maintenance.

Like Lake View to the south, the plans of early developers like Martin Van Allen would have been stillborn without commuter trains. From the very beginning in 1868, when Van Allen's Ravenswood Land Company snapped up 164 acres of virgin forest and farmland, the developers cut a deal with the Chicago and Northwestern Railroad guaranteeing at least seventy-five commuters a day if the railroad would build a new stop. Van Allen and his associates hoped the $7.20 fee for one hundred rides would attract only wealthier commuters. To sweeten the pot, the developers even built the Sunnyside Inn, hoping that visitors to the resort would want to stay as residents. Many did.

The advent of streetcars and the extension of the elevated line in 1907 opened Ravenswood to the less affluent, who poured in, transforming the once-bucolic suburb with an array of small houses, two-flats and multi-unit apartments.

Today's transit battles continue but this time over whether to continue bus service on Lincoln Avenue, one of Ravenswood's oldest and busiest streets. Just days after Abraham Lincoln's assassination, Little Fort Road, as it was then known, reputedly became the first street in America named in honor of our murdered sixteenth president. While the German presence remains in the form of businesses like the Brauhaus and Merz Apothecary (one of the city's few homeopathic drugstores), the Niedersachsen athletic club

Introduction

and DANK (German-American National Congress) Hall, the old Teutonic influence is slowly being nudged aside by Thai eateries, yoga studios and the Old Town School of Folk Music, reportedly the largest school of its kind in the entire country.

Part I
LAKE VIEW

WATERFRONT LIVING AT ITS BEST—AND STRANGEST

It was 1837. In England, Queen Victoria began her sixty-four-year reign, Isaac Pittman published his first shorthand book and Charles Dickens's *Oliver Twist* was becoming a bestseller. In Germany, Fredrick Froebel opened the first kindergarten, to the dismay of Prussian authorities, who favored less permissive teaching methods, while in France, Louis Daguerre developed the first successful photography process.

Over here, a financial panic in New York resulted in $100 million in bank losses; the American Peace Society condemned all wars and called for a Congress of Nations with a World Court to resolve future international disputes; novelist Washington Irving coined a new phrase in his book *The Creole Village* by referring to "the Almighty Dollar, that great object of universal devotion"; Chicago evangelist Dwight L. Moody was born in Northfield, Maine; abolitionist Elijah Lovejoy was murdered by a pro-slavery mob in Alton, Illinois; and Chicago officially became a city, where C.D. Peacock opened what is now Chicago's oldest business.

Swiss-born Conrad Sulzer—the first white settler in what is now the Lake View community—arrived in Chicago to find a population that had grown from 150 to 4,170 in just four years, saw the possibilities and bought one hundred acres from Chicago's first mayor, William Butler Ogden, near what is now Montrose and Clark. The nearest town of any size, Kenosha, Wisconsin, could be reached only by Little Fort Road (which was renamed

Above: Hotel Lake View, an early lodging house.

Left: Conrad Sulzer, Lake View's first permanent white settler.

Lake View

Lincoln Avenue only a week after the sixteenth president's death). The only other land link to the outside world was Green Bay Road (now Clark Street, originally a trail laid out by General Winfield Scott between Fort Dearborn and Green Bay, Wisconsin, during the War of 1812).

Over the next decade or so, Sulzer got rich selling land to well-heeled Chicagoans fleeing a major cholera epidemic. By 1855, Sulzer was Lake View Township's first assessor, and he sold one of his huge tracts to Graceland Cemetery and the Ravenswood Land Company, which was made up largely of a group of ex–Civil War vigilantes organized to protect the city against a feared escape of Confederate POWs from Camp Douglas on the South Side.

Sulzer, however, never really left his original homestead. After his death of an apoplectic seizure on Christmas Eve 1872, the old pioneer was buried in Graceland Cemetery, not far from where he lived after first coming to Chicago thirty-five years earlier. Sulzer also gave his name to today's North Side regional library at 4455 North Lincoln Avenue, which replaced the fifty-year-old Hild branch, ironically named for an early library commissioner who'd been fired partly because he didn't believe in branch libraries.

The Sulzer influence continued through Conrad's son Frederick, who followed his father into the floral and landscape business, was elected Lake View town clerk in 1867 and became highway commissioner the following year and town supervisor in 1875.

The Montrose Avenue Bridge about 1910.

For sixteen years, Frederick Sulzer served on the township board of education, and he is credited with installing the area's first water purification station near what is now Montrose Avenue and Marine Drive. That waterworks remained until the 1970s, when it was razed to make way for a Cuneo Hospital expansion project.

The younger Sulzer died in 1892, ironically the same year Sulzer Road, once bordering the north end of his property, was renamed Montrose Avenue for reasons never made clear. His wife continued to live in the still-standing landmark mansion he built at 4223 North Greenview well into the 1940s. After his daughter, Grace, the last of the family, died in December 1957, the property was donated to Trinity Seminary and Bible College for use as a student residence. But the school soon sold Sulzer Hall and moved to suburban Bannockburn after the adjacent property became too high-priced for the college to expand.

The Sulzer influence, however, is far from dead. For over half a century, the Sulzer Foundation, created from Grace's $120,000 estate, has provided grants to scores of local church, community and social service organizations. In one year alone, $151,000 was distributed to sixty-eight recipients including the Neighborhood Boys and Girls Club, the Lincoln-Belmont Pantry and the Ravenswood–Lake View Historical Association.

Chicago Temple Chimes Still Honor Early Settler John Turner

Next time you hear the chimes of the Chicago Temple at Washington and Clark wafting through the Loop, think of Lake View pioneer John Turner.

The set of bells was donated to the Methodist cathedral back in 1935 by William Turner as a memorial to his father. A member of the Old Settler's Society and the exclusive Calumet Club, John Turner came here from England exactly a century earlier and built a house and livery stable just across the Chicago River on the Near North Side. In 1859, like Conrad Sulzer before him, Turner bought his eighty-eight acres of Lake View township land from Mayor Ogden and leased the tract to a farmer, who immediately built a house on what is now the northeast side of Addison and Wolcott.

After being burned out by the Chicago Fire twelve years later, Turner relocated his tenant and took over the farm himself. He raised sheep, pastured cattle and stabled horses and helped found the First Methodist Church of Ravenswood a few blocks away.

Lake View

The Turner House on the 1800 block of Addison sheltered refugees during the 1871 Chicago Fire.

Some years later, as the city built up around his farm, Turner sold forty acres of his holdings to Samuel Eberly Gross, the amateur novelist and real estate developer who made a fortune selling the same kind of wooden houses in Lake View that had been banned in Chicago after the fire. A handbill distributed by Gross in 1883 promoted $700 to $1,000 lots in the Lincoln/Wellington/Lakewood Triangle just three blocks from the end of the Lincoln Avenue horse car line "where there are no city taxes."

In 1907, another part of what was once the Turner Farm at Byron and Western became the Selig Polyscope Company, Chicago's first movie studio, where early thrillers like *The Adventures of Kathleen* were made.

William Turner lived in the family house until 1946, and the landmark was razed about a dozen years later to make way for a new home for then-alderman Charlie Weber, who died there under still-disputed circumstances less than a year after moving in.

John Peter Altgeld:
Heroic Rags to Riches to Rags Story

Another immigrant buried not far from Conrad Sulzer in Graceland Cemetery went from being one of the richest men in Lake View to a near pauper.

John Peter Altgeld's holdings once included the tract bounded by Lincoln, Belmont and Greenview, which would eventually become Chicago's second-biggest retail area; a home at Arlington and Clark; and an early skyscraper at 131 North Dearborn, where he once rented office space to Clarence Darrow.

Then he became governor and his fortunes went downhill. By the time Altgeld left office, he was not only nearly destitute but probably also the most despised politician in a state where there was plenty of competition for that honor. During his days in Springfield, he was burned in effigy, crucified on editorial pages, frozen out of public functions and even denied the traditional right to make a farewell speech at his successor's inauguration. "Illinois has had enough of that man," incoming Governor John Tanner explained after dropping Altgeld from the program.

Altgeld's "crimes" had nothing to do with the $2 million he'd honestly accumulated during a lifetime that included service in the Civil War, a stint as a Missouri prosecuting attorney, a once-lucrative law practice and six years as a Chicago Superior Court judge.

Even his enemies grudgingly conceded that if Altgeld had waited a few months to be born here instead of Germany, he probably would have beaten out William Jennings Bryan for the 1896 Democratic presidential nomination.

But Altgeld lost everything almost overnight when he pardoned the three surviving Haymarket "conspirators" after concluding they'd been wrongly convicted with falsified evidence before a rigged jury controlled by an openly biased judge. To add insult to injury as far as the powers that be were concerned, Altgeld then tried to keep President Grover Cleveland from sending in federal troops to break the generally orderly 1894 Pullman strike. The man who would be hailed in years to come as the architect of the Illinois public school system, early champion of women's rights and promoter of the secret ballot was being called an anarchist, "apologist for murder" and a few other choice names we can't use here.

By the time he died just minutes after speaking at a 1903 rally in Peoria supporting the Boers against the British in the South African War, about all Altgeld had left was a home on the 4500 block of North Malden and a plot in Graceland Cemetery. But even that grave was neglected for years until a group of admirers finally collected enough money to repair the monument and replace the bronze plaques thieves had pried off the marker.

Lake View

Ironically, one of the speakers at the 1974 rededication ceremony was then-governor Dan Walker, who later became one of a string of Illinois governors to do jail time on corruption charges.

North Side's Own "Valley of Kings" Was the "Living End" for Many

Just a few years after Graceland Cemetery's groundbreaking in 1861, suburban Lake View officials began worrying that the dead would soon outnumber the living. By 1867, the future "Valley of the Kings" had expanded from 86 to 275 acres after Chicago passed a new law barring burials inside the city limits, forcing the relocation of hundreds of bodies from what is now the south end of Lincoln Park. The move was accelerated when high water levels in the lakefront cemeteries began causing putrefying corpses to "pop" to the surface, causing a grave health problem.

Lake View township officials, however, complained that Graceland had already grown to the point where the graveyard's "continued presence mars the enjoyments of the living because it is pernicious to health and life itself."

Cemetery supporters, on the other hand, argued that Graceland "had become a garden where Grace, Beauty and Light render less somber the solemn associations of the tomb. We lay the bodies of the beloved dead in the bosom of Mother Earth and they become part of her substance.

"They return to dust, and from thence spring flower and leaf and waving grass," said an especially flowery editorial.

Lorado Taft's iconic statue of "Death" or "Eternal Silence" guards early settler Dexter Graves near the entrance of Graceland Cemetery. *Photo by Patrick Butler.*

The eternal Palmer House of Potter and Bertha Palmer in one of Graceland Cemetery's most exclusive neighborhoods. *Photo by Patrick Butler.*

A report issued by Graceland trustees conceded that "a portion of the grounds are now low and unsightly" but added that "had they not been purchased by our company, it is likely they would never have been devoted to anything more picturesque than a cabbage garden."

Trustee Bryan Lathrup eventually reached a compromise with Lake View authorities under which Graceland would take thirty-five more acres to the east. Graceland, in turn, surrendered everything beyond its original eighty-six acres, part of which became Wunder's Cemetery on the south side of Irving Park Road.

While the dead at Graceland, Wunder and St. Boniface Cemeteries probably did indeed outnumber the community's living at one point, all that changed after the 1871 Chicago Fire. By 1883—six years before Lake View officially became a city—the suburb's population had grown to nineteen thousand, at least partly because the blue-collar tradesmen pouring into Chicago were prosperous enough to demand decent housing but couldn't afford the all-brick construction required by Chicago's "fireproof" building code.

Lake View

Lake View Joins Chicago—and Not Everyone Is Cheering

In 1889, when apartments around Belmont and Ashland were renting for five dollars a month, Chicago annexed Lake View—along with Jefferson, Lake and Hyde Park townships—quadrupling the size of the city literally overnight.

Shortly after annexation, developers began snapping up nearby farms, built cottages on 25- by 125-foot lots and offered free horse car rides to prospective buyers of the $2,500 model homes on the Cubley "outskirts" of town around Lincoln and George. That area had already become a predominantly blue-collar neighborhood, mainly because of the cluster of meatpacking plants built to furnish meat for Civil War troops, including those stationed at Camp Fry, a recruit depot and later POW camp near what is now Clark and Diversey.

"In this one blow, Chicago almost achieved its present status," former Illinois governor William Stratton remarked at a July 15, 1989 annexation centennial celebration. The annexed area includes thirty-four of Chicago's fifty wards and fifty-two of the city's seventy-seven recognized community areas, historian Richard Bjorklund said.

But not everyone in Lake View was jumping for joy at the idea. In what was then the city of Lake View, the vote was 2,503 for annexation, 1,999

Employees from the Cubley Drum Factory at Wolcott and Wilson in 1889.

against. Many, like Mary Brown, were having major misgivings about becoming Chicagoans. "Personally, I'm a little reluctant about the changes, as we have been so well satisfied with our own municipal government and its headquarters at Town Hall [Addison and Halsted]," she wrote in her diary after the city council approved the annexation ordinance. "Time will tell, of course…but I doubt whether things will ever be the same again."

In that same diary entry, however, Ms. Brown wondered out loud whether women would ever get the vote and a voice in matters like annexations: "I do not suppose it's possible, but once in awhile I rebel at the old idea that I am forbidden the right to vote just because I am a woman."

Not everyone was as genteel in their dissent. Right after the Chicago City Council and a majority of Lake View's voters approved the annexation, Lake View mayor William Boldenweck seized his suburb's records and funds and barricaded himself in his town hall office until he was forced to back down by the Illinois Supreme Court. It was just another quirky chapter in the thirty-eight-year-old German immigrant's turbulent life.

At the height of the Civil War, Billy Boldenweck tried to enlist in the Union army but was rejected because he was only thirteen. Undaunted, he

Lake View's first town hall, replaced in 1907 with a police station that still goes by the same name.

Lake View

A crowd watches a 1920 fire at Lincoln and Newport.

An 1888 view of Paulina Street between Belle Plaine and Berteau Avenues. A notation on the back of the photo says that thanks to the new kerosene lanterns in the middle of the block, "it will no longer be necessary to carry a lantern to find the way home on nights when the moon does not shine."

tried to join the navy by stowing away on the USS *Michigan* during a stop in Chicago but was discovered and sent home before the gunboat weighed anchor. A year later, he dropped out of school to become a tinsmith and then worked as a clerk in a hardware store for six years before finally joining his brother's stonecutting business, which he bought in 1875.

The Chicago Telephone Company at 3522 North Sheffield, 1906. Lake View's first phone exchange grew from three hundred subscribers in 1906 to ten thousand a decade later.

But despite Boldenweck's resistance to annexation, it had become painfully obvious to just about everyone that smaller communities like Lake View could no longer support the ever-growing array of fire, police and educational services demanded by the voters. Boldenweck's bullheadedness, however, didn't keep him from eventually becoming president of the Chicago Drainage Board or serving as assistant director of the U.S. Sub-Treasury office here from 1906 to 1910.

Samuel Gross's Business Included Eighteen Towns, Cyrano Novel

During his lifetime, Samuel Eberly Gross is said to have sold 44,000 lots, built 7,500 homes and created eighteen suburban villages like Gross Park, a one-time cabbage patch located between Diversey, Belmont, Damen and Ravenswood Avenues. But that's really not how the scientist and inventor of "mathematical instruments" wanted to be remembered.

Back in the early 1900s, the aspiring playwright spent much of his reputed $4 to $6 million fortune trying to prove that French poet Edmund Rostand's play

Lake View

Claremont Avenue looking south from Sunnyside in the fall of 1904.

Chanticleer was nothing more than a cheap ripoff of Gross's novel *The Merchant Prince of Cornwall*, which Gross wrote in 1896 and had 250 copies printed up. When the sensational trial finally ended, Gross was awarded one cent in damages and the judge ruled that Rostand's play was never to be performed in the United States, an order later overturned by a higher court.

Born in 1843 in Pennsylvania, Gross moved west with his parents when he was three. After service as a captain in the Union army during the Civil War, he ended up in Chicago, where he studied law. By 1883, he was urging would-be homeowners to take the Lincoln Avenue streetcars beyond the city limits to Wellington and Southport Avenues. There, he promised, they could build wooden houses and not have to pay city taxes.

Children shoveling snow on the 3400 block of North Oakley, early 1900s.

The next year, he laid out the Gross Park subdivision, which included forty-five acres bought from the Turner family, whose homestead at Addison and Wolcott stood until 1959, when Charlie Weber bought the property. Lots in this "ideal subdivision" were sold out of offices near Lincoln and Belmont and in the Loop for an average of $900 apiece, with $100 down and $10 a month for five years at 6 percent interest. Houses in Gross's developments across the North Side ranged from $1,600 for a cottage in the Avondale area a few miles northwest of Lake View to a more substantial seven-bedroom Gross Park home for about $3,500.

Later, he would model the landmark Alta Vista Terrace development in Wrigleyville between Grace and Byron on a lane he saw during a visit to London. The forty houses, featuring twenty different designs, are each built to match the house diagonally opposite at the other end of the street.

He contributed land for two still-active local schools, Hamilton and Audubon; contributed property for numerous Lake View churches; rarely foreclosed on a mortgage; and did everything he could to make homeownership within the reach of almost everyone.

By the time he died, virtually bankrupt as a result of his legal battle with Rostand, there would be a Gross Park Hotel at Lincoln and Roscoe, a Gross Hall community center at Belmont and Ravenswood and even a Gross Park Community Church at Addison and Hamilton. But the Gross Playground on the 2700 block of West Lawrence Avenue was named for longtime

Campbell & Simpson Blacksmith Shop, at what is now 1523 West Belmont Avenue, about 1889.

park commissioner Theodore Gross. No relation. After all, even the man who vanquished the man who claimed to be Cyrano de Bergerac's creator couldn't have everything.

Today, of course, monthly rentals on a typical Lake View/Ravenswood apartment are about what it would have cost to buy a house in Gross's day. In 1888, when John Heim opened what he always insisted was Lake View's first real estate office at what is now 3148 North Ashland, homes near Lincoln and Wellington were going for anywhere from $400 to $1,100. Landlords like furniture maker/undertaker Christian Krauspe were renting four-room flats for $8 a month. Two rooms at the rear of Krauspe's frame building at 1628 West Belmont could be had for $4.

Heim himself bought up what was once a truck garden near Lincoln and Belmont owned by Daniel Steinbeck, who had always bragged about how that parcel would someday be the hub of a vibrant commercial district. Within two years of moving here in 1880, however, Steinbeck was dead of typhoid, gone too soon to see how right he was.

Streetcars, Trains Pulled It All Together on the Early North Side

Just as the automobile built the suburbs, Lincoln-Belmont-Ashland owed much of its early prosperity first to the railroad and then the streetcar.

When North Side railroad historians fondly recall the Graceland Dummy, they're not talking about some legendary village idiot but the small stem line that first linked Chicago to Lake View. From 1870 until the late 1880s, the three-car train made three trips a day from Fullerton Avenue and Clark Street up Broadway to Byron Avenue and the lakefront, west on Irving Park to the entrance of Graceland Cemetery. The three-mile trip reportedly took about fifty minutes.

For those who didn't have their own wagons or carriages (and most didn't), the "Dummy Line," so called because it was pulled by a small, relatively quiet engine, was the only link between the Chicago city limits and places like Lake View Town Hall at what is now Addison and Halsted, Lake View House on Byron and the lakefront or Graceland, Wunder's and St. Boniface Cemeteries, where many families regularly picnicked.

Commuters from downtown took a Clark Street horse-drawn omnibus (an intra-city stagecoach that was later replaced by a sixteen-passenger

This Dummy railroad, shown here in an 1870-era photo, was the first commuter service between the suburb of Lake View and downtown Chicago.

A 1903 view of the Chicago, Milwaukee & St. Paul Railroad's Sheridan Park stop at Wilson and Evanston Avenue (now Broadway).

Lake View

Train tracks approaching the Wilson Avenue railroad station in the early 1900s.

"bobtail" car) from the Loop. From there, they transferred to the Dummy Line or the horse-drawn streetcars that went up Lincoln Avenue to Belmont, where wagon traffic had to pass a toll gate to go on to "country" towns like Bowmanville (just north of today's Lincoln Square) or Niles Center (now part of still-suburban Skokie).

When Samuel Gross started selling his lots, one of his main selling points was that the new subdivision was only three blocks from the end of the car line, with an extension planned all the way to Belmont Avenue. As far back as 1870, cable cars from downtown had been going as far north as Fullerton (then the city limits), where commuters boarded horse-drawn omnibuses for the rest of the trip to Lincoln and Belmont.

Every fall, the open yellow "summer cars" were replaced with enclosed coaches filled with straw to warm the commuters' feet. Of course, if the horses slipped and fell on the ice, male passengers were expected to jump up and help the conductor get the horses back on their feet.

Mass transit in those days wasn't just inconvenient, it was dangerous—sometimes so much so that William Stead, in his 1894 book, *If Christ Came to Chicago*, noted the "multitude of mutilated people," victims of streetcar and railroad mishaps who supported the large artificial limb and crutch industries.

By 1900, what the Lake View residents used to call the "Main Line" was finally running all the way up Lincoln to a turntable at Ashland Avenue. The improved

Construction of elevated tracks at Sheridan and Irving Park roads, 1902.

The last horse car on Evanston Avenue (Broadway), early 1900s.

service suffered a major setback a year later when two hundred cars in the barns at Wrightwood and Sheffield burned in a fire started by an overheated stove.

Trolley cars stayed in service here until 1906, when Charles Yerkes of the Chicago Street Railway Company introduced the electric trolley. By 1913, the fares had been raised from a penny to an unheard-of five cents. Transit officials called that the price of progress. Some things never change.

Lake View

WHEN A FEW RIVERVIEW REVELERS LITERALLY DIED LAUGHING

When Wilhelm Schmidt, owner of a popular German bakery on Clybourn Avenue, bought an abandoned brickyard on Western and Belmont in the late 1800s and turned it into a picnic and shooting range for his family and friends, he never expected his Sunday afternoon retreat to grow into Chicago's largest and longest running amusement park. Over the next sixty-three years, thousands of patrons came to "laugh their troubles away," as the ads said.

Around 1904, Schmidt put in some swings and a few rides just to keep the women and children occupied while the men shot skeet. Not long afterward, Schmidt's son, George, returned from Europe with some ideas he'd picked up visiting places like Copenhagen's Tivoli Gardens. By 1908, Wilhelm Schmidt had installed a custom-made carousel with seventy hand-carved horses, and a few years later, he built a ballroom and ice-skating rink for the winter season.

As the 1920s roared in, Riverview was open to the public, especially the drinking public. During Prohibition, Riverview continued providing beer despite frequent raids by federal agents and visits by the rival Capone and O'Banion gangs, which each wanted sole distribution rights.

By the 1920s, the first roller coasters were being installed, making Riverview a place where generations of boys became men, testing their courage on death-defying rides like the sixty-five-mile-an-hour Bobs, where a 150-pound man weighed 15 pounds at the top of the "hill" and 400 pounds going down the eighty-five-foot drop. Built at a cost of $85,000, the Bobs carried 1,200 riders an hour, consistently attracting some 700,000 riders per season right up until 1967, the year the park shut down.

The Bobs were scary but nowhere near as dangerous as some of the earlier rides like the Jackrabbit and the Big Dipper, which "not only looked dangerous but were dangerous," a longtime patron recalled. In 1921, a navy officer from Great Lakes Naval Training Center north of Chicago was killed when he tried to stand up in the Dipper. An envelope maker fell off that same ride four years later, and still another patron was thrown from his seat the following summer.

Three men died in 1935 on the Pippin, which injured at least twenty-two riders two years later when it ran out of speed at the top of a ramp and plunged backward, crashing into an oncoming coaster. It was enough to give the Pippin a "good" reputation with would-be daredevils and get the ride shut down as a threat to public safety.

Not long afterward, Riverview roustabouts were fined for hanging a few rowdy patrons by their thumbs. But worse flak came in the early 1950s when anti-cruelty groups went bananas over the monkey races featuring small apes in miniature cars careening around a track. The attraction, popular as it was, never reopened after a mysterious 1953 fire.

Besides the legendary Bobs, considered in its day "the most fearsome roller coaster in the country," and other rides like the Pair-O-Chutes, made famous in a 1965 song by the Beach Boys on their *Summer Days and Summer Nights* album, Riverview had its equally memorable sideshows. Among them were hourly reenactments of the Civil War battle between the ironclads *Monitor* and *Merrimac* and the World War I newsreels reportedly smuggled into the United States by U-boats to keep the local German population abreast of the Fatherland's latest triumphs.

A generation later, thousands of Nazis marched through the park during the American National Socialist Party's 1939 picnic. Just down the street, neighbors could hear Hitler's rantings broadcast via loudspeaker from Haus Vaterland near Byron and Western. The cops were called more than once by non-Aryans annoyed at having their sleep disturbed so rudely.

Even Mayor William "Big Bill" Thompson came under fire from assorted reformers for giving the city's public school children a day off classes to be his guests at the park. A spokesman for the Illinois League of Women Voters complained that His Honor already had "abundant opportunities to give Chicago children recreation combined with wholesome education without sacrificing valuable school hours." A proposal to build Lane Tech High School right next to Riverview drew still more criticism a few years later.

During the 1930s, Riverview was hard hit, not only by the Depression, but also by a devastating fire that destroyed the Bug House and part of the Derby roller coaster. To attract cash-strapped customers intent on "laughing their troubles away," the Schmidts introduced a host of innovations like foot-long hot dogs.

Black/white friction at Riverview heightened in the 1940s and '50s. The "Dunk Bozo the Clown" game, where contestants threw a ball at a target that would drop a man into a water tank, was changed to "Dump the Nig---r." Blacks were hired to sit over the tanks and taunt any white passersby. By the time the attraction closed under pressure from the NAACP, the "African Dip," as it had been renamed by then, was arguably the highest-grossing concession in the park's history. The black men who lost their jobs, incidentally, had reportedly been making more than $300 a week.

Dumping the "Dip," however, apparently didn't put a damper on seething racial tensions. By the 1960s, Riverview had hired its own police force to keep order. Some Chicagoans insist it was the racial animosity that caused owner George Schmidt to shut down the park at the end of the 1967 season when Riverview, with thirty-three rides, was still making as much as $65,000 a day.

But usually reliable sources thought it was just a case of Schmidt getting an offer he couldn't refuse—an estimated $6.5 million from a developer who promptly razed the park. In its place are police facilities and courtrooms, DeVry University, Clark Park and a shopping mall with two supermarkets. The antique seventy-horse merry-go-round is now at Six Flags over Georgia in Atlanta, and the distortion mirrors from the Aladdin's Castle fun house are reportedly in a Palatine nightclub.

Over the years, Riverview was also the scene of special events like a speech by Industrial Workers of the World leader "Big Bill" Haywood to eighty thousand supporters and the 1924 launch by another "Big Bill": a ship funded by Mayor William Hale Thompson for a "scientific" expedition in search of flying fish in the South Seas. Thompson left the ship halfway down the Mississippi, and the ship itself was sold for scrap in New Orleans. The very cynical suggested that the project was nothing more than a publicity stunt to keep the temporarily out-of-office Thompson in the public eye until the next election. It wasn't the first time the self-styled "Cowboy Mayor" made headlines. A few years earlier, in a bid for the Irish and German vote, "Big Bill the Builder," also known as "Kaiser Bill," not only threatened to punch England's King George V if he ever set foot in Chicago but also ordered the public libraries to toss out any "pro-British" books.

Never at a loss for a gimmick, the very wet mayor fueled his 1927 campaign with a rally aboard the Fish Fans floating clubhouse in Belmont Harbor. The 1,500 supporters who turned out for the kickoff event stomped their feet so hard the converted schooner sprang a small leak. Within minutes, the revelers found themselves treading six feet of water despite His Honor's earlier assertion that the Fish Fans was the driest club in town. The controversial club had been swamped with problems almost since its founding by Thompson and some friends in 1922, ostensibly to promote the propagation of fish in Illinois waterways to help feed poor children.

The club, in fact, seemed far more synonymous with moonshine than its avowed goal of "putting sunshine in the life of the barefoot boy" after Prohibition agents found gallons of booze in the members' lockers. The members themselves, however, were never prosecuted, supposedly because the club's bookkeeper swallowed the list of names just as the feds were coming through the door. During the trial, Mrs. Arthur Gordon, one of the members, swore she'd never seen anything wetter in the clubhouse than the children's bathing suits. Others testified that the members were busy enough holding "Barefoot Boy picnics" that drew as many as four thousand urchins. The jury ultimately found the restaurant concession operation guilty of liquor trafficking but acquitted the club itself of public nuisance charges.

The club's critics, however, charged that Big Bill's calls for members to "stand by the ship" really meant standing by Thompson's beleaguered political organization. Thompson won the election, but "the ship" soon went under, literally as well as figuratively, despite repeated attempts to bail it out. On September 5, 1928, the Fish Fans held their last meeting before the old schooner was taken away by creditors and scuttled in the middle of Lake Michigan.

But reformers' angst over real or imagined goings-on at the Fish Fans club wouldn't be the last time allegations of illegal gambling got Riverview dubbed the "Monte Carlo of the Midwest." They charged that games like the Wheel of Fortune were rigged and that the operators were taking money from the workingman and giving it to "mysterious owners" who, not surprisingly, were never found.

About all that's left to remind anyone the park ever existed is a *Riverview* sculpture near the front entrance of the police complex.

HARMS PARK WAS AN ALMOST NONSTOP PICNIC FOR FIFTY-FOUR YEARS

Just down the block from Riverview, everyone from the German Schwaben Verein to St. Patrick's Day revelers partied at the privately owned Harms Park on the northeastern corner of Western and Berteau from 1893 to 1946, when the five-acre site was sold for housing for returning World War II veterans.

Although it's been more than half a century since the almost weekly bouts of *gemultlichkeit*, a few longtime Lake View residents still recall the twenty-four-horse merry-go-round, beer gardens and bratwurst stands that catered to everyone from the Old Settlers' Club's 1937 picnic marking Chicago's centennial as a city to neighborhood residents on a Sunday afternoon stroll.

Owned since 1857 by founder Harry Harms's family, the property originally extended all the way to Lincoln Avenue and was converted into a picnic grove by Harms, a farmer, building contractor, legislator, highway commissioner, postmaster and founder of Niles Center (now Skokie, a suburb just north of Chicago). As if that weren't enough, when he wasn't siring eleven children, the prolific Harms developed Lincoln Avenue (then known as Little Fort Road) as a plank toll road from suburban Morton Grove

Lake View

The home of brewer Valentine Busch on the southeast corner of Clark and Diversey with the Ferris wheel from the 1893 World's Fair in the background.

to Halsted and Fullerton, once the city limits. He died at age eighty-two in 1914, never living to see his picnic grove's busiest year, 1921, when ninety-seven different organizations met there, compared to the usual forty to fifty picnics per season.

A Henry Harms descendant, Albert Harms, was still living on the grounds with his wife and mother in 1946 when he sold the property to developer Arthur Zimbroff and moved to St. Petersburg, Florida. Then fifty-seven, Albert Harms told a reporter for the local Lerner Newspapers at the time that he planned to spend about a year "loafing" before getting back into business, "preferably in the electrical line.

"I'm much too young to start rusting," he explained.

As Harms went south, a number of German and Irish groups tried to buy or lease the eastern end of the tract, but those talks eventually petered out. The carousel was sold to a carnival, and the Schwaben Verein moved its picnics to Kolze Park, out by Narragansett and Irving Park, not far from the county poorhouse and asylum.

Zimbroff then built a thirty-two-lane bowling alley, a four-hundred-space parking lot and the Oakley Gardens, which featured twenty-nine homes on 32- by 125-foot lots. The homes were being sold for $12,650, with veterans getting priority. More than one hundred neighbors heartily endorsed the project at a meeting called by Alderman Frank Hilburn (47th Ward) to get support for a necessary zoning change, but not before Hilburn himself first mourned Harms Park's passing. "I know how many old-time residents of the ward feel a personal loss with the closing of Harms Park," he said. "I have even wondered where I would hold future picnics for my neighborhood."

Ultimate "Party Animal" Charlie Weber Left Plenty of Questions

One of the most memorable Lake View politicians, however, was the inimitable Charlie Weber, remembered even today for his "Kids Day" at Riverview and making his 45th Ward the only one in the city with its own flag. While he was at it, he also installed ashtrays at selected bus stops in the Lincoln-Belmont-Ashland shopping district. He personally ordered dog owners to pick up their doggies' doo and was probably the first Chicago elected official to call for laws requiring owners to clean up after their pets.

"I know the dogs can't read. It's not their fault. It's their owners," said Lake View's own *burgomeister*, who was occasionally seen chasing down litterbugs in his Bavarian lederhosen while driving a $6,000 street-cleaning machine he bought with his own money. He also opened seven neighborhood play lots at his own expense, which were taken over by the Park District after his death.

So it was no surprise to friends who say nobody ever found a "fortune" from Weber's real estate and insurances businesses, taverns, ice cream parlor, Riverview concessions and even his own newspaper, the *Lake View Independent*. Weber spent money almost as fast as he made it, usually on others, said admirers, who also disputed allegations that Weber ran the ward's bookie operations. "Charlie Weber never placed a bet in his life, although some of the people around him may have," said the now-deceased Michael Lerner of the Lerner Newspaper chain, adding that while Weber did make the best beer on the North Side during Prohibition, he probably kept the gangsters out of the neighborhood.

Not that Lake View completely escaped the terror of the times. In 1933, a reputed Al Capone flunky, Gus Winkler, was shotgunned outside a beer

Lake View

distributorship allegedly run by Weber at 1414 West Roscoe, although Weber was never charged. "It was probably Bugs Moran [a Capone rival] who did that," another neighborhood businessman recalled in the late 1980s. "Weber's guys didn't kill anyone. Ever."

But any mystery surrounding Charlie Weber only deepened after his death in August 1960, when he and his wife, Emma, were found dead of carbon monoxide poisoning in their home on the old Turner property. Police found a car engine running in a downstairs garage.

The deaths were ruled accidental despite rumors of a murder/suicide. At a political function a week earlier, someone had reportedly heard Mrs. Weber—convinced that the alderman had a mistress—tell her husband, "Charlie, if I can't have you, nobody will." While that story has never been confirmed, others believe Weber may even have been a victim of his own clout. According to one story, Weber and his builders may have ignored a code requirement that the garage ventilation be designed so the fumes went outside, not upstairs. To this day, some longtime ward residents still believe a building inspector may have looked the other way.

Most of what was left of their estate (including an apartment building on Ashland Avenue and a yacht in Palm Beach, Florida) went to Weber's longtime sidekick, Renee Clayton, who led more than 1,700 other mourners to a double funeral at St. Andrew's Church, where Bishop Bernard Sheil minced no words about his old friend. "Charlie Weber was no saint," Sheil noted at the end of his eulogy. "May his time in Purgatory be short."

Ironically, Weber is the only Chicago alderman whose visage once adorned a church—the front stairway of St. Alphonsus—for reasons nobody was ever able to explain. Undoubtedly just another mystery wrapped in an enigma.

Given the old *burgomeister*'s penchant for making things like bank accounts disappear, nobody was especially surprised when a giant photo of Weber unaccountably vanished moments after it had been donated by 44th Ward Democratic Committeeman John Merlo during a luncheon marking the twenty-fifth anniversary of Weber's death. It has never been seen again.

Guardsmen Went After Pancho Villa as Practice for Great War

Back in the late 1960s and early '70s, yells of "Hell no, we won't go" often shook the rafters of the old Kingston Mines Coffeehouse at 2356 North

Sergeant Charles Hope at home in Lake View during the 1898 Spanish-American War.

Lincoln, then a favorite haunt for North Side hippies and peace activists. Ironically, the last time there were that many people in the old First Illinois Field Artillery armory was probably the week of June 20, 1916, when hundreds of local men were doing a dress rehearsal for World War I by going after Mexican bandit and self-styled revolutionary Pancho Villa, who jumped the border and killed several Americans during a raid on Columbus, New Mexico.

Captain Frank Course of the 3500 block of Janssen, the battery commander, eventually had to call in police to remove the crowds of well-wishers, curiosity seekers and would-be volunteers like the guy whose enraged wife stormed into the armory, claiming her husband told her he'd been kidnapped and pressed into service. Another man came in explaining that he was to be married that evening but would postpone the nuptials if he were allowed to sign up. Others hastily married—like Lieutenant Richard Dunne, who wed Frances Fitzgerald of the 3500 block of North Pine Grove in a private ceremony in his family's home—while Captain A.F. Siebel wed Mrs. Anna Knudson of the 4400 block of North Magnolia at the Buena Presbyterian Church just before reporting for duty.

Lake View

Not far away, at the First Cavalry Armory on Clark Street, the nineteen-year-old son of Judge (later baseball commissioner) Kenesaw Mountain Landis enlisted without incident. Up in Ravenswood, however, the seventeen-year-old son of Police Captain Thomas Gallery (of the same Gallery clan that produced three navy admirals in World War II) was having a hard time assuring his mother that he wouldn't lose an eye or an arm.

Another local officer, Major M.M. McNamee, also of the First Cavalry, refused to be left behind even after a buckboard he was riding to Union Station collapsed at Clark and Division, sending the horse fleeing in sheer panic. Although badly cut, McNamee grabbed his baggage, hailed a cab and caught up with his outfit at the railroad depot, where a medic patched him up while his troops waited to get aboard their train for Springfield.

By July 4, the local boys were off to San Antonio, Texas, to join the largest U.S. force to take the field since the end of the Civil War sixty years earlier. They returned home three months later without ever finding Villa's gang.

But not to worry. Lake View resident and Illinois lieutenant governor Barrett O'Hara assured officers of the First Illinois Provisional Regiment, which had been left behind, that neither Pancho Villa nor the already-raging war in Europe was all that important. The real trouble, he predicted, would come soon enough from Japan.

FIRST WORLD WAR'S FRONT LINES RAN DOWN "LINCOLNSTRASSE"

World War I's Western Front didn't end in France. The battle lines were also being drawn right here, where in 1914 one-third of Chicago's 600,000 Germans (most of them living in Lake View) signed a resolution pledging Austrian emperor Franz Joseph and Germany's Kaiser Wilhelm "our unchangeable love of home and Fatherland." For some, lip service wasn't enough. Soon after the outbreak of the war, dozens went down to the German consulate on the Near North Side to enlist in the Kaiser's army.

During those first three years before the United States entered the war, the Germans were joined by many Chicago Irish, who saw the war as a chance for the Old Sod to finally win freedom from England. Not far away from Lake View, twenty thousand Poles (whose homeland had been partitioned

Hundreds of workers turned out during this World War I bond rally at International Harvester's Deering Works.

more than a century earlier by Russia, Austria and Germany) turned out for a rally supporting the Allies at St. Mary of the Angels Church on North Wood Street.

Things began to change in early 1917 after the discovery of a telegram sent by German foreign minister Count Arthur Zimmerman promising Mexico the return of the American Southwest if Mexico were to attack the United States.

The previous summer, the First Illinois Field Artillery, based on Lincoln Avenue and made up largely of Lake View residents, had been sent after Mexican bandit Pancho Villa. Although the infamous desperado was never captured, many of the National Guardsmen called up for the four-month campaign formed the nucleus of the first officer training camps after the United States declared war on the Central Powers in April 1917.

Most North Siders soon forgot their differences once America entered the so-called War to End All Wars in a kind of dress rehearsal for an even more agonizing trial by fire that would again briefly pit neighbor against neighbor a generation later.

Lake View

ARMISTICE SENT NEIGHBORS POURING INTO STREETS TO CELEBRATE, FIGHT

When word reached Chicago shortly after 1:00 a.m. on November 11, 1918, that the guns of World War I had finally fallen silent, Lake View—like the rest of the country—ran amok with joy and didn't settle down for at least a day. One self-described "shoutin' Methodist" called it "the most glorious event since the birth of Christ" on hearing the news on a North Side elevated train. "I'm all fussed up about it."

Even twenty-seven-year-old David Mulligan of the 1300 block of West Wellington quickly got over his disappointment at having to sit out the fighting, although his draft number—258—had been the first one pulled by Secretary of War Newton Baker some seventeen months earlier. The Bowman Dairy milkman had registered with the rest of his neighbors at the Fullerton/Southport Selective Service office but was deferred because authorities felt his wife and two small children would have had a hard time getting by on a private's pay of twenty-one dollars a month. "I think we were all more stirred up than during World War II," Mulligan would recall years later. "European affairs were pretty much of a mystery to us and it made people gasp to think of going overseas to fight a war."

Not far away from the Mulligan home, "Victory Baby" Walter Wentzlaff was born on the 2600 block of Wellington just as the neighbors started pouring out into the streets to celebrate the end of 584 "meatless, wheatless" days.

By midday, things had gotten so wild that Mayor William Hale Thompson had been asked to shut down the saloons in the interest of public sanity. But even that outspoken opponent of the war, who'd been hanged in effigy along the lakefront just a few months earlier for accurately describing Chicago as "the world's seventh-largest German city," refused to do anything as drastic as closing saloons. "Kaiser Bill," as Thompson was sometimes derisively called, had earlier clashed with Illinois governor Frank Lowden over a permit the mayor had issued for an antiwar rally. Lowden had threatened to call out the National Guard to break up the protest, and Thompson vowed to use Chicago cops to resist if necessary. But the pacifist meeting came and went while the two politicians were still arguing. Thompson, nevertheless, preferred to keep a low profile during the victory reveling.

Throughout the day, at least thirty-five men with black eyes were hauled into the East Chicago Avenue lockup for getting just a little too exuberant in the local taverns. The next morning, Judge John Richmond asked the miscreants if they'd had a good time. "Yes," he mused before anyone could reply. "It was a glorious day, and I guess you all better go home and be good."

At about that same time, William Wrigley, who'd just become a major shareholder in the Chicago Cubs baseball club, was predicting a great 1919 season now that mainstays like pitcher Grover Cleveland Alexander would soon be coming back to work.

Of course, not everyone shared the spirit. Fred Buhle, seventy-five, of the 2000 block of North Fremont, who'd served in the Prussian army back in 1866, was among the last in the war to be arrested for making seditious statements. He not only claimed Germany had every right to go to war but also predicted that the Kaiser, who'd just abdicated and fled to Holland, would someday regain his throne.

Newspaper editorials warned that just because the shooting had stopped was no excuse for people like Buhle not to watch what they said. After all, the Land of the Free was going to stay that way even if it meant that sauerkraut had to be rechristened "Liberty Cabbage" and the German Hospital renamed Grant Medical Center.

And just to make sure there were no misunderstandings, the Goethe statue at Diversey and Sheridan was "redone" in red, white and blue by a band of local patriots.

Twenties Roared through Lake View Despite Prohibition, Recession

The 1920s that followed the Great War were anything but the "return to normalcy" promised by newly installed President Warren G. Harding.

A young collage graduate named Louis Lerner had just opened a newspaper—the *Booster*—that would eventually become the flagship of what was for a time the world's largest newspaper chain. But by then, the area didn't need much boosting as the population shot from 60,535 to 96,482 in just ten years and the Lincoln-Belmont-Ashland intersection was well on its way to becoming Chicago's busiest shopping district outside the Loop.

Men's shoes, hats, seven-inch dinner plates and cigars were going for $1 apiece at the new Wieboldt's department store at Lincoln and School. A live show, *Peg O' My Heart*, was playing at the Victoria Theater at Belmont and Sheffield, while Alice Mayson and the Marigold Follies were headlining at

Lake View

The Lincoln-Belmont-Ashland intersection, once Chicago's third-busiest commercial strip, around 1918. The Wieboldt's Department Store building, shown here under construction, was converted to luxury condos in the mid-1990s.

Broadway and Grace. *Dr. Jekyll and Mr. Hyde* was playing at the Vitagraph at 3153 North Lincoln Avenue from 1:00 to 11:00 p.m., while Blanche Sweet was starring in *The Deadlier Sex* at the Bugg Theater at Lincoln and Robey (later Damen Avenue). You could rent a five-room furnished apartment at 3450 North Southport for $65 a month or buy an eight-room house in Ravenswood for $11,500.

But times weren't so good in the aftermath of the Great War. Unemployment skyrocketed—there were 160 applicants for every 100 job openings—and Chicago Health Commissioner John Dill Robinson had to warn that landlords who failed to supply heat in the winter would be charged with murder if residents died as a result.

Prohibition was only about a year old, but Canadian whiskey disguised as "soap" was already flooding Chicago during the summer Al Capone turned twenty-one. Because the Canadian "soap" was fetching as much as $105 per case, nobody was shocked to hear that some police officers were being investigated for allegedly selling $30,000 worth of stolen whiskey to the Rainbo Gardens nightclub at 4814 North Clark Street.

Lake View Marked Fiftieth as War Again Broke Out in Europe

In October 1939, neighbors were mourning the death of Cardinal George Mundelein and found themselves again choosing sides as war broke out in Europe. But they still found time for a week-and-a-half-long festival marking Lake Views's first half century as part of Chicago.

About one thousand local children marched in a torchlight parade led by a thirty-five-piece Catholic Youth Organization band from St. Alphonsus Church, followed by girls in one-horse shays (two-wheeled carriages once popular for running errands). To lend atmosphere, they even had cows munching hay on the curbs around Lincoln and Belmont.

That same week, political boss Charlie Weber and his brother, Clarence, officially dedicated a bronze plaque honoring their late father outside Weber Hall, 1411 West Oakdale, while members of National Guard Signal Corps units unveiled the latest in battlefield communications. Hundreds turned out for the show, and some even enlisted in the army on the spot. For despite protests of neutrality by the White House, few doubted it was only a matter of time before Uncle Sam again joined the fighting in Europe.

Local Germans Took the Lead in Wartime Bond Drives

Less than a generation later, Lake View residents geared up to fight another war to end all wars—once again after some hard soul-searching in the usually easygoing German community. Before Pearl Harbor, there were bitter divisions over whether Adolph Hitler deserved German-American support, neutrality or opposition.

Local bunds began openly marching up Lincoln Avenue, loudspeakers blasted Der Fuhrer's speeches from Haus Vaterland near Roscoe and Western and Riverview Park was given over one evening for a mini-Nuremberg-style rally. "German generals like [Erwin] Rommel were heroes to a lot of kids around here," recalled neighborhood newspaper publisher Michael Lerner, one of the organizers of the Lake View Council on Religious Action in 1940 to help offset a mounting pro-fascist mood. As one repentant local Nazi supporter later explained, anything seemed better than the chaos following Germany's 1918 defeat.

Lake View

But all that changed overnight after Pearl Harbor.

Production rallies were staged at plants like Stewart-Warner and Appleton Electric. Wieholdt's department store hosted bond drives featuring local headliners like the Maloney Family Band from St. Andrew's Parish, and the Lincoln-Belmont YMCA held twice-monthly USO dances. Hundreds of radios were dropped off at the Lerner Newspaper office on Greenview for donation to American GIs around the world, and housewives baked cakes and even went to the train stations to pass out combs, soap and toothbrushes to departing troops.

Among those leading efforts on the homefront were realtor Harry Starr, tailor George Iberle and politician Joe Gill, who paid for all USO parties at the Lake View Center near Clark and Belmont out of his own pocket.

Meanwhile, the crucial Norden Bombsight was being developed at Victor Comptometer near Rockwell and Irving Park. And the Elks at Diversey and Sheridan Road, the only civilian organization in the entire country selected to recruit construction specialists for the military, met its quota three months ahead of schedule.

Some forty years later, Lake View's Zum Deutchen Eck Restaurant would host a historic reunion where eleven surviving crewmen of the

This memorial made by the neighbors around Belmont and Oakley is a continuing reminder of the community's role in World War II. *Photo by Patrick Butler.*

German submarine *U-505* were fêted by forty-five of the American sailors who captured them off the North African coast during the first boarding operation of its kind since the War of 1812. The former enemies drank a toast to the late Admiral Daniel Gallery, the Ravenswood native (and one of three brothers who became admirals) who made the decision to try taking the sub and its crew alive.

The next day, the still-grateful Germans paid a visit to their old ship, now on permanent display at the Museum of Science and Industry. But some of the aging guests drew the line at going to a showing of *Das Boot* (The Boat), a movie about German submariners then playing at the Lake Shore Theater. "Living through it once was enough," a former petty officer explained.

HITLER KIN SOUNDED WARNING ABOUT UNCLE DURING VISIT TO TEMPLE

While the German-American Bund was still very active in Lake View in November 1939, it wasn't rolling out the red carpet the day Adolph Hitler's nephew paid a visit—possibly because William Patrick Hitler, who considered his famous uncle a dangerous psychopath, was the featured speaker at a forum sponsored by Anshe Emet Synagogue at 3760 North Pine Grove on "What the German People Are Thinking."

Of course, the twenty-eight-year-old Irish-born son of Bridget Dowling of Dublin and Alois Hitler, the Fuhrer's half brother, had little love for his dad's side of the family even before Uncle Adolph came to power. For openers, the father deserted the family when William Hitler was only three to go back to Berlin, where he opened a restaurant that later became a favorite haunt of many top Nazis. Things got even worse after Hitler's takeover for William Patrick, who had planned on becoming an accountant. He said he was eventually forced to live in Germany for several years because his last name made it impossible to find a job anywhere in England.

Although he claimed to have known many of the Third Reich's movers and shakers, William Hitler (or "Paddy" Hitler, as he was known in England) apparently didn't meet the future Fuhrer in 1928 and saw him for the last time shortly before the Nazi takeover five years later.

Though he insisted he'd never been a party member himself, the Errol Flynn lookalike said conditions in post–World War I Germany were so desperate that it was understandable most Germans initially backed Hitler, who said he would never have been elected if England and France had treated the Weimar Republic better. "But now, by his persecution of Jews, Catholics and other minorities, his medieval barbarism and his sellout of those who backed him have made his downfall inevitable," the estranged nephew said during his visit here.

He added, however, that at the time it seemed unlikely Hitler would be allowed to plunge Europe into another major war since it appeared the German people were essentially peace-loving and still smarting from the trauma of the Great War. "If there is a blowup in Germany, it will come from within the Germany Army rather than the ranks of the people," William Hitler said. "These Army leaders who are fundamentally intelligent must know Hitler is leading them to national suicide."

It took five more years, of course, for William Patrick Hitler's predictions to materialize. When a nearly successful coup attempt finally did come on July 20, 1944, it was led by a group of top-ranking *Wehrmacht* officers, including the legendary Field Marshal Erwin Rommel, a one-time Hitler protégé.

This speech was quite a switch from William Patrick Hitler's earlier attempts during a trip to Germany before the war to get his uncle to give him a high-ranking job with the regime. He eventually worked for a time in an Opal auto factory and sold cars and later escaped back to England and the United States. It took an OK from President Franklin Roosevelt himself to allow William Hitler to join the U.S. Navy, where he served as a medical corpsman and was wounded once.

After his discharge, he changed his last name, settled in Queens, New York, ran a medical testing business out of his home and had four sons. Rumor has it they may have made a pact to let the Hitler bloodline die with them. In any case, none of them had children.

North Side's Own "Benedict Arnold" Didn't Get Away with It

On the other hand, it was probably hard to muster much empathy for a traitor like Herbert Haupt, the one-time Lane Tech High School ROTC cadet turned German saboteur. The twenty-two-year-old was one of eight enemy agents brought by Nazi U-boats to the coasts of Long Island and Florida. The fifth columnists were to blow up as many U.S. defense plants as possible with the help of German-supplied explosives, more than $90,000 in

Men and women march in formation during an event at the Social Turners sometime in the early 1900s. The German American athletic and educational organization had its clubhouse at Belmont and Paulina.

cash and a list of local Nazi contacts that included Haupt's own uncle, Walter Froehling, at 3623 North Whipple. Incredibly, Haupt was about to get his old job back at Simpson Optical Co. at 3200 West Carroll Avenue—makers of the crucial Norden bombsight—when FBI agents finally caught up with him on June 27, 1942. About a year earlier, he'd reportedly gone to Mexico, sailed for Japan with a German passport and then took a blockade runner to Germany, where he was trained as a saboteur.

Haupt, who had come here at age nine with his family, claimed he'd returned to Germany to visit relatives and insisted he was only trying to flee Nazi agents when he was caught by the feds. U.S. investigators were especially skeptical after several of Haupt's former acquaintances described Haupt as a "sneering runt" who often boasted of how Aryan "supermen" like himself would someday rule the world. Even his ex-fiancée, Gerda Miland, whom he'd met in 1940 at Haus Vaterland, a local Nazi Bund clubhouse, ended up testifying for the prosecution, some say under government pressure.

On August 9, after a semi-secret military trial—the first of its kind since the Civil War—Haupt and five of the other enemy agents died in a Washington, D.C. electric chair.

Three weeks later, Haupt's parents, who'd been arrested for hiding their son in their home at 2235 North Fremont, were themselves indicted for treason along with Froehling and his wife and Mr. and Mrs. Otto Wergin, whose son had reportedly defected to Germany with the younger Haupt. By November 14, Federal Judge William Campbell had sentenced the three men to death and their wives to twenty-five years imprisonment and $10,000 fines. The penalties were later commuted.

Some, like Miland, thought Haupt and his parents may have been little more than dupes. "I'll never believe he meant to go through with the [sabotage] plan," she told reporters after learning of Haupt's death.

But after Pearl Harbor, that mood quickly changed. Other generals like Dwight Eisenhower and George Patton became the new idols of Lake View youth. Haus Vaterland went dark, and the only rallies at Riverview were to sell U.S. war bonds or promote recruitment.

Enola Gay's Bomb Bays Blew Cover Off Local Soldier's Secret

For Clara Christian of the 2100 block of West Bradley Place, news of the atomic bombing of Hiroshima on August 6, 1945, explained a lot. Like why her son Richard always avoided talking about where he was stationed or what he did. Or why the army kept sending the twenty-two-year-old NCO to school instead of overseas like almost everyone else. Mrs. Christian eventually started to think they were simply saving her son for the future occupation of Japan.

She was taken aback when Richard asked for a copy of George Joos's *Theoretical Physics* for his May 15 birthday. But then Richard and his brother Russell, who was then an Annapolis midshipman, had always been math geeks. The mystery deepened when Sergeant Christian told a friend during one of his rare leaves that he didn't have much laundry to worry about because his coveralls were always burned after two or three wearings.

It was only the day after the bombing that Christian—along with the other seven thousand Manhattan Project workers at Los Alamos, New Mexico—was finally allowed to call home and tell his folks what he had really been up to for the previous two and a half years. He had been trained as an army pharmacist's assistant and assigned to lab jobs, first at Oak Ridge, Tennessee, and later at "Lost Almost," as the secret reservation at Los Alamos, New Mexico, was called by those who worked there. While there, Christian witnessed at least one of the tests held to make sure the A-bomb would work.

It did.

It worked so well, in fact, that even though he had once edited the newsletter the Lerner Newspapers used to publish for its newsboys, Sergeant Christian was at a loss for words when he tried to describe what he saw. "He finally told us just to watch the newsreels and look at the pictures in *Life* magazine," Mrs. Christian said, recalling how her son had told her how those witnessing the experiment were warned to wait several seconds before looking at the explosion. Many who didn't look away were temporarily blinded by the flash from the blast, Sergeant Christian recalled. Christian himself shielded his eyes as ordered, kept his sight and got two job offers—one from the University of Illinois and the other from a lab in California—even before he was released from the army.

Mrs. Christian recalled that she probably should have realized her son was up to something when the FBI questioned a neighbor about him a few years earlier.

V-J Day Brought Cheers, Tears on Lake View Streets

"They started it, neighbors end it," cheered the headline of the August 19, 1945 edition of the Sunday *Booster*, Lake View's neighborhood newspaper.

On the streets back home, reaction to news of the war's end ranged from elation to prayerful reflection. "The greatest threat to world freedom has been obliterated," said U.S. representative Alexander Resa (D-9th Ward) when contacted by reporters at his home on the 3600 block of North Pine Grove.

For William Hart of the 3100 block of North Lincoln Avenue—the father of four sons fighting in the Pacific—the victory was very personal. "I thank God it's all over. I've been praying for this for a long time," he said.

Credit for the victory also went to everyone from one-time *Booster* delivery boy Walter Koblenz, who had just won the Bronze Star in the Philippines, to Julie Novak and five of her co-workers at Press Wireless at 1339 West Diversey. A front-page story told how Novak, Minnie Finkler, Florence Vanderhoof, Dorothy Lass, Susan Fagan and Winnie Bromley each donated a pint of blood every ten weeks and worked every Tuesday evening rolling bandages at the local Civil Defense office at 2433 North Lincoln.

But as dedicated as they were, Novak and her friends weren't the area's champion blood donors on the local homefront. That honor probably went to Ray Washer of the 2800 block of North Orchard, who had given seventeen pints over the previous three and a half years. One of the last people to qualify for the blood drive's Two-Gallon Club was a woman appropriately named Harriet Flood of North Kenmore Avenue.

By war's end, the neighbors had contributed 43,102 cakes, 5,719 cartons of cigarettes, 4,200 pounds of candy and 5,100 pounds of cookies to local servicemen's centers.

The annual Harvest Picnic at Harms Park became an impromptu victory celebration organized by Schwaben Society secretary George Iberle, who ran the bond drives and seemingly most other war-related activities in Lake View.

But the war wasn't quite over for Lake View Bank executive Oliver Cox and fifty-one other members of North Side draft boards who had been told not to shut down operations just yet. Local Civil Defense units were put to work helping to ease the transition in West Lake View factories from war production to consumer goods.

One of the first to benefit from "reconversion" was Art Krause's bakery at 3114 North Lincoln Avenue. Now that the war was over, Krause said one of the first things he planned to do was get a new oven. But patrons would continue having to take numbers just as they had during the war. Krause started the practice when rationing curtailed the supply of butter, which often meant there were not enough freshly baked rolls to go around every morning. Customers got so irate that "some of them were even cussing the girls out," Krause said.

For others, victory had come too late to celebrate. Grief-stricken over the loss of his soldier son, Arthur Kopp Sr. of the 1200 block of West Oakdale shot himself in the head less than a week after the Japanese surrender. And the Lerner Newspapers' V-J Day edition carried word that another former *Booster* newsboy, John Gorman of the 1900 block of West Wolfram, had been one of the last GIs killed in the Pacific.

In the end, victory carried a high price for everyone.

FOR SOME, D-DAY REENACTMENT FIFTY YEARS LATER WAS FAR TOO REAL

Despite 46th Ward alderman Helen Shiller's futile efforts to block a fiftieth-anniversary reenactment of D-Day on Montrose Beach on June 6, 1994, arguing it would create too many traffic and crowd-control problems, some 450 reenacters in authentic World War II battle gear stormed ashore from five assault craft as fifteen vintage aircraft, including a B-25 bomber, "softened up" 100 or so "German" defenders holding the beachhead.

Chicago's World War II Commemoration Committee, the U.S. Navy and the Historical Reenactment Society had worked for the previous year to make the largest D-Day commemoration this side of France as realistic as possible. They needn't have worried. The event at times turned out to be far more realistic than anyone planned. Like when one of the navy landing crafts had to unload its "troops" in at least five feet of water that proved so rough one man lost his rifle. Or when a smaller boat ferrying the "British" and "Canadian" contingents started taking on water.

It was déjà vu all over again for Walter Kallas and hundreds of other veterans who had been there for the real D-Day. Back in 1945, Kallas, who later became owner of a grocery on the 3600 block of Montrose, was a staff sergeant with the Ninety-second Chemical Mortar Battalion. The Bronze Star recipient not only survived the Longest Day but also went through four other major battles, including the Bulge.

He counted himself especially lucky to have been there for the reenactment. After all, not long after Normandy, the army offered him a choice between a promotion to second lieutenant or a thirty-day leave. Kailas took the leave and said that when he reported back, he found 75 percent of his outfit had been wiped out.

Warren Berry, a Chicago policeman when he wasn't a chief warrant officer in the navy reserves, had professional reasons for going along for a ride on one of the landing craft. The amphibious assault specialist assigned to a unit at Great Lakes Naval Training Center said that if the Normandy landings were taking place in 1996, the casualties would be a lot lighter because the landings would be done much differently, with helicopters and hovercraft nobody even dreamed of fifty years earlier.

Others on the boats, like Sam Henner of Ritchfield, Ohio, predicted that World War II may someday be as popular with reenactors as the Civil War. "But not now. Not enough time has passed yet," Henner explained. "The memory's still too fresh in too many people's minds."

When deValera Won One for Irish Freedom at Wrigley Field

Another struggle for liberation—and the debut of lights at Wrigley Field—came to Lake View the night of July 19, 1919, when Irish freedom fighter Eamon deValera addressed a throng of forty thousand supporters. The New

Lake View

York–born provisional president of the newborn Irish Free State was making his first tour of the United States to win support for the controversial treaty partitioning Ireland between the Free State and British-occupied Ulster.

Earlier in the day, deValera had been greeted by ten thousand well-wishers at the LaSalle Street railroad station and then whisked to a visit with Colonel Richard O'Sullivan-Burke, a veteran of both the U.S. Civil War and the 1867 Fenian uprising in Ireland, at 833 West Fletcher.

After Mass at St. Vincent's Church at 1010 West Webster, the one-time death row inmate named by the British as one of the ringleaders of the 1916 Easter Rebellion in Dublin received an honorary law degree from Reverend Francis McCabe, DePaul University's president, who praised the mathematics teacher as "the embodiment of everything we require of our students—devotion above all to principle."

Later, deValera was fêted by former Illinois governor Edward Dunne, who recalled how during a visit to Ireland before independence, "I found 700 English jails and every one was full, with maybe 12 or 15 prisoners who were real criminals."

While introducing deValera, Dunne noted, "A pig in Armour's [meatpacking plant] has more chance to live to a ripe old age than the Irish had to realize their ideals under British domination." America, on the other hand, is different, said deValera, "for because the national soul of your country is pure, you have trodden on no peoples."

Consummate politician that he was, however, deValera steered clear of any criticism of President Woodrow Wilson's policy of seemingly supporting every freedom movement but Ireland's, noting only that he had no doubt Washington would "do the people's bidding once they find out what they want."

Earlier, in 1889, the Irish troubles had played a role in the still-unsolved grisly murder of Dr. Patrick Cronin, whose naked body—stripped of everything but a religious medal—was found stuffed in a sewer near Broadway and Foster. Police know the forty-three-year-old Irish American political activist had his head bludgeoned to a pulp in a house on Ashland near Cornelia.

Although four men were convicted of the murder (with one freed after a second trial), nobody ever confessed. And nobody could ever agree on a possible motive. One theory was that Cronin was about to blow the whistle on an embezzlement scheme involving top leaders of the Clan-na-Gael, a secret Irish revolutionary group. Another was that Cronin had simply been executed for being a paid British informer by one of the Irish nationalist groups operating in Chicago.

Also a mystery is why the killers who stripped Cronin of his clothes, hoping to make identification harder, left an easily traceable holy medal. Lake View mayor Boldenweck, however, surmised that the killers were obviously "too religious" to go that far.

March 17, 1948:
The Night the Music, and Anne Hunt, Died

Chicago's Irish eyes stopped smiling for a long time after March 17, 1948, when a dance floor collapsed during a St. Patrick's Day party at Lake View Hall at 3233 North Clark Street, leaving one woman dead and nearly one hundred people injured. At about 10:10 p.m., a 58- by 104-foot section of the third floor gave out under the weight of six hundred revelers at the Connaught Social and Athletic Club's annual bash.

To Michael Lynn, "It sounded like the drums of the band were playing a long roll. The floor started sloping and I lost my balance and fell."

Margaret McHugh, twenty-four, was just walking off the dance floor with her date, Ray Studeman, twenty-six, when they slid down to the second floor "as if we were being sucked into a pit."

Downstairs, twenty-seven-year-old Susan Plaske heard the loudspeaker announcing, "We will now cease bowling," followed by a terrible scream as the ceiling started falling in.

Bartender John Kelly heard a cracking sound and ran to the other side of the room just in time to avoid being crushed to death like Anne Hunt, thirty-five, whose body would remain pinned under debris for the next few hours as rescuers focused on trying to save the living.

Investigators would later credit several dozen men—some of them off-duty police and firemen—with keeping panic and injuries to a minimum by forming a human chain to help the stunned partygoers climb back up through the rubble to the third-floor fire escape. Firemen helped some two hundred people down ladders while police dropped ropes to those still caught on the second floor.

Within hours after the collapse, investigators learned not only that landlord John Jenkins didn't have a license for a dance hall but also that the building was never designed to safely accommodate one.

Lake View

LAKE VIEW HIGH'S TEACHERS WROTE THEIR OWN LEGENDS, THEIR WAY

Lake View High School, reputedly the oldest continuously operating secondary school in the entire state, likes to boast about alumni like actress Gloria Swanson, author John Gunther and ventriloquist/Charlie McCarthy creator Edgar Bergen. But what about teachers like the Page brothers or James Norton?

Back around the late 1890s, Benjamin Page, who taught Latin, left to promote a dandruff "cure" that made him a millionaire several times over. His brother, William, also a Latin teacher, supposedly went prospecting for oil in the Peruvian jungles and, according to one account, "is believed to have been the victim of cannibals."

Then there was the science teacher James Norton, dimly remembered for one of the most heroic "rescues" in the school's history. During an 1885 fire that destroyed the original campus, Norton was seen dashing recklessly into the flames, only to emerge a few minutes later with what looked like the charred remains of a student. But according to an old yearbook account, "gasps gave way to relieved smiles when closer examination revealed the skeleton was only 'Johnny,' an expensive specimen from the science laboratory whose bones they had often counted as part of their classwork." Professor Norton eventually became Lake View's principal.

The school itself had been built in 1874 on land at Ashland and Irving Park Road donated by Graceland Cemetery with the stipulation that the building cost no more than $15,000 and be completed within two years.

The original Lake View High School No. 1, once known as the "Dummy Road School" because it was located on the route of the Dummy trains linking Lake View with the Loop.

Although seventy-five students applied when the school opened in 1874, only eight were considered able to do the work. The four-member faculty included the principal, Augustus Nightengale, who made the metric system required knowledge.

Less than a year after the 1885 fire, Nightengale opened a new two-story building for 250 students. Within ten years, enrollment had grown to 800. In 1913, a new record was set when 475 graduates got their diplomas, and by 1916, Nightengale's building was replaced by a new four-story complex. In 1939 (with an enrollment of more than 4,500), a final addition left the school as it stands today.

A Lake View High School diploma, by the way, didn't come easy. Just getting admitted was a character builder, thanks to an entrance exam personally designed by then-superintendent Albert Lane. Students taking the 1878 admission test were expected to be able to draw a map of South America, including all the rivers and mountain ranges; list the exports of Rio de Janeiro, Brazil, and Liverpool, England; locate Marseilles, Quito, Mount Aetna and the Orange River on a map; and give a "synopsis" of the verb "run" in the indicative and potential modes, interrogative form and first person, singular number! And while they were at it, aspiring Wildcats had to find the cubic root of 62,588,123 and explain how to figure out the time differences between two places once they knew the longitude of each.

Applicants had to know everything from the metric system to penmanship, along with "the elementary principles of prosody." Nobody got in without correctly answering at least 70 percent of all the questions on the test and being able to spell words like Pentateuch, colloquy, antipathy and requisition. According to the school's annual report, even students not bound for college had to take Latin prose composition during a four-year course "designed to prepare a person for the ordinary vocations of life."

While local students paid no tuition, anyone from outside the city of Lake View paid twenty dollars a year or fifty cents a week.

Lane Tech, Like Its Namesake, Was a Mix of Brains and Brawn

A North Side school that was once turning out more people who went on to get PhDs than any other in the Chicago Public School system was named for a principal and Chicago school superintendent who wasn't as old as many of

Lake View

his students when he became Chicago's youngest-ever high school principal at age seventeen. Albert Grannis Lane brought a unique combination of brains and brawn to the job back in the late 1850s, when Franklin School at Sedgwick and Division was having a discipline problem. Some of the rowdier students had taken to chasing unpopular teachers out into the street and finally even dumped the principal himself into a snowdrift. Lane was asked to take over even without a high school diploma. The board of education decided he had all the right qualifications just the same.

So in 1908, nobody was especially surprised when they put a state-of-the-art vocational school where Franklin Elementary once stood and named it after Lane, whose top priority even as Chicago school superintendent had been the development of a manual arts program. Freshman classes at the new school included carpentry, wood turning and cabinetmaking. Sophomores got molding, foundry, forge and welding. Juniors took machine shop, and seniors got electric shop, the school's most advanced course.

By 1915, Lane had a daytime enrollment of 2,500 and 6,300 night students taking everything from dressmaking and heating and ventilating to advertising and salesmanship. The new school was a success almost from the start—so much so that Lane outgrew its old home and moved to Western and Addison, just down the block from Riverview, in 1934. On opening day, September 17, more than 7,000 boys met at Wrigley Field and walked the two miles or so to the new building.

By the 1920s, students were publishing a four-page daily newspaper and a fifty-page monthly magazine and boasting a 250-member glee club. They had long since overflowed into six branch schools and sixty portable classrooms.

The Depression forced cutbacks in plans for an expanded campus that was to have included an elementary school, junior college, football stadium and baseball diamonds, running track and fifteen tennis courts. The 700,000-square-foot building put up with federal WPA funds opened in 1934 and turned out to be one of the biggest high school campuses in the country, with 214 classrooms and shops surrounded by twenty-one grassy, tree-lined acres and three and a half miles of walkways.

During World War II, Lane not only sent 8,700 graduates off to fight but also maintained an active Civil Air Patrol (Air Corps civilian auxiliary) squadron and sold $3 million in bonds—enough to buy six ambulances and two B-17 Flying Fortress bombers. During their classes, the school's shop students made small boats for the navy and gliders for pilot training.

Lane became a selective admissions school in the late 1950s, right after the Russians launched the world's first space satellite. It has provided the

Chicago Symphony Orchestra with at least fifteen musicians and at the same time racked up fourteen Illinois High School Association athletic titles.

Alumni include singer/songwriter Frankie Laine, who reportedly took his stage name from his alma mater; former Bill Clinton White House aide John Podesta; actor Adrian Zmed (*T.J. Hooker*, *Dance Fever*); TV talk show host Steve Wilcos; Phil Cavaretta, who led the Chicago Cubs to the 1943 Divisional Championship; and Air Force general Donald Kutyna, a 1951 graduate who headed the U.S. Space Shuttle program after flying 120 combat missions as a fighter pilot in Vietnam.

Girls finally came to Lane in 1971 despite protests from 1,500 boys who picketed the school board, warning that the overall quality of education would deteriorate. It didn't, of course, though some faculty members like veteran teacher Pat O'Malley warned in the late 1980s that with female enrollment approaching 40 percent, Lane could someday be considered a "girls' school."

So much, some feared, for old Albert G. Lane's legacy of brains and brawn.

Olympic Legend Avery Brundage Made a Lasting Mark Here

If you want to know all about Avery Brundage, go visit 3325 North Lincoln Avenue. That's the last thing he built before leaving town to begin a sixty-year reign as czar of the International Olympics Committee (IOC).

Although his Olympian career was compelling enough for a 1988 TV miniseries, the building contractor himself had nearly forgotten it all by 1972 when he finally got around to discussing the 3325 building's early history in a letter to longtime Lake View businessman and civic activist Harry Starr. That letter, in fact, was evidently one of the last Brundage wrote before being ousted as head of the IOC following the slaughter of eleven Israeli athletes by Arab terrorists during the Munich games.

It was a far cry from Brundage's earlier triumph in that same city when he stood up to Adolph Hitler himself, who'd tried to keep Jews from participating in the 1936 games. But no sooner had he put the German Fuhrer in his place than he stripped Jesse Owens—hero of that Olympiad—of his amateur status after learning that Owens had accepted $40,000 for racing against a horse. If there was one thing Avery Brundage believed in, it was the sanctity of amateur sports and the strict separation of sport from commerce and politics. He was so annoyed by the growing practice of putting advertising

Lake View

on the skis of competitors in the Winter Olympics that he seriously proposed cancelling the Winter Games, or at least the Alpine skiing events.

He couldn't have picked a worse time to be president of the IOC. During what passed for the post–World War II peace, there were two Germanys, two Chinas, two Koreas and the problem of apartheid in South Africa. Although he survived one of the most turbulent eras in Olympic history, it was his comments at the memorial service for the eleven murdered Israeli athletes during the 1972 games that finally did him in. When several African nations boycotted that year's Olympics, an outraged Brundage compared that snub to the massacre itself—and within six days was removed as IOC president.

He died at eighty-seven two years later in Bavaria, Germany.

Brundage—the first IOC president to have personally taken part in the Olympics—competed in the decathlon and pentathlon during the 1912 Olympics in Stockholm, where he was bested by Jim Thorpe, whom he also later stripped of his gold medals after learning that Thorpe had once played semi-pro basketball. Even his enemies agreed that Brundage insisted on following everything to a logical conclusion.

Except, perhaps, his 3325 North Lincoln building. The four-story pie-shaped landmark at Lincoln and Marshfield was originally supposed to have been nine stories high but was sold early to Marshfield Trust and Savings shortly after Brundage left Chicago.

Starr, who had been a vice-president of that bank when it folded during the Depression, bought the building and kept it for nearly fifty years until his 1977 retirement. When he wasn't tending to business, he was leading World War II bond drives, raising funds for the local YMCA and waging a winning fight to save the Paulina CTA station. The last time he made news was a year after his retirement, when burglars broke into the safe deposit boxes in the currency exchange he ran next to his insurance and realty office. Within a few months he was dead, hit by a truck not far from his Skokie home.

Longtime residents still call Brundage's half-finished bank building "Harry Starr's Place."

1896 "Great Race" Wasn't Much to Write Home About

If you thought the automobile age began in Detroit, auto racing got started in Indianapolis or motorcycles have always been little more than gas-powered bikes, you'd be wrong on all counts. America's love affair with the car probably started getting serious on November 28, 1895, when the country's first major auto race sped through Lake View and the competing vehicles were being called "motorcycles" (as opposed to "horseless carriages").

The Great Thanksgiving Day Motorcycle Race was the brainchild of Herman Kohlsaat, then editor of the *Chicago Times-Herald* and an early auto enthusiast at a time when cars were considered little more than rich men's toys. Kohlsaat himself laid out the racecourse from Jackson Park, up Michigan Avenue and Sheridan Road to Calvary Cemetery in Evanston, down Clark Street and Ashland Avenue to Roscoe Street, down Western Avenue to Belmont Avenue, Belmont to Milwaukee Avenue and back to the Midway.

But the competition was a near disaster almost from the start. Originally set for November 2, the race had to be postponed several weeks because not enough of the cars had arrived in Chicago. Automotive pioneer Henry Ford, for example, wanted to enter one of his early vehicles but couldn't get anyone to loan him the train fare here. Another car sponsored by Macy's department store in New York had to be shipped by rail after it got stalled in a snowstorm in Schenectady.

By the end of November, a number of those cars that made it here withdrew from the race rather than try to compete in heavy snows and sixty-mile-per-hour winds. By 9:00 a.m. on race day, only six cars had showed up. Within three hours, the driver of a Benz entered by a New York refrigerator company had to be brought to the finish line in a horse-drawn buggy, and two electric cars were sidelined when their batteries went dead. The Macy's car dropped out after colliding with a streetcar, hitting an overturned carriage and then damaging a wheel after an encounter with a cab.

Soon, all but two cars—a Motor Wagon driven by pioneer auto designer Frank Duryea and a Benz piloted by Decatur, Illinois brass goods manufacturer Oscar Mueller—had dropped out of the competition. As the cars passed Western and Belmont, Mueller's passenger, Charles Reid, collapsed from exposure and had to be sent back to the hotel on a sleigh. When Mueller himself later fainted, an umpire who had been riding with him took the wheel and brought the car to the finish line—and a $1,500 second prize.

Duryea, who won the $2,000 first prize, sold thirteen of his Motor Wagons the following year. His cars stayed on the market until 1917.

The next day, the American Motor League (forerunner of groups like the Chicago Motor Club) was founded to lobby for better roads.

Lake View

But the most important outcome of the race, as far as some participants were concerned, was that American-made cars like the Duryea were beginning to overtake foreign makes like Benz. It would only be a matter of time, they predicted, before U.S.-made autos were the envy of the world.

"Where's the Beef?" Cops Wondered in Spring of 1897

Ironically, Captain Hermann Schuettler, who investigated the Patrick Cronin murder discussed earlier, was also a key figure in what was briefly touted as Lake View's "Crime of the Century," the spring 1897 murder of Louisa Luetgert, whose husband, Adolph, apparently bludgeoned her to death.

Police concluded that Adolph and his wife were arguing over the sausage maker's teenage mistress before Luetgert dumped the Missus in a rendering vat, where Schuettler noticed a wedding ring engraved with the initials L.L. (for Louisa Luetgert). An employee had even seen Luetgert stirring that bubbling cauldron throughout most of the night. When the new shift started for work the next morning, they found their boss sleeping in his office and the vat overflowing with a foul-smelling brownish goo.

When Luetgert went to the Sheffield Avenue station to report that his wife had been missing for several days, Schuettler remembered him as the same man who had been so hysterical a few months earlier when his dog got lost. Schuettler poked around the plant, where he found not only the ring but also a piece of human bone at the bottom of the vat.

Luetgert and his lawyers argued that since there was no body, there could be no murder charge. But States Attorney and future U.S. senator Charles Deneen insisted that the greasy blob he brought into court and passed among the jurors on sheets of butcher paper was all that was left of Mrs. Luetgert.

Luetgert was found guilty but spared the gallows because several jurors remained uneasy about the lack of a corpse, despite assurances by Judge Joseph Gary (the same judge who presided over the Haymarket Trial) that a body wasn't necessary for a conviction in this case.

"She'll come back and you'll see what fools you've been," said Luetgert, claiming his wife had just run away.

In a way, he was right. She did come back, said Luetgert, who died in Joliet Prison three years later complaining that his wife wouldn't leave him alone. After Luetgert's death, her ghost supposedly found its way back to the old house, where new tenants eventually got so alarmed by spectral apparitions that the building was eventually moved around the corner.

Not surprisingly, the case left such a bad taste in people's mouths that the sausage plant went belly up soon after Luetgert's arrest. The building on the 1700 block of Diversey later served as a still during Prohibition, a woolen mill and a factory that at various times made barstools, pinball games, slot machines and airplane propellers.

Yet long after the case was nearly forgotten, rope-skipping youngsters were still singing:

Old man Luetgert made sausage of his wife
He turned on the steam and she began to scream
"There'll be a hot time in the old town tonight."

Arabs, Jews Still Pray for This Christian Couple a Century Later

At the other extreme were Horatio and Anna Spafford, still remembered today in Jerusalem, of all places, where at least one congregation of Yemenite Jews still prays for the wealthy Lake View couple who sold everything, started an evangelical sect and moved to the Holy Land after their four daughters died in an 1873 shipwreck and a son died of scarlet fever five years later. Overcome with grief, Horatio Spafford wrote the poem that eventually became the much-loved Protestant hymn "It Is Well with My Soul." The Spaffords reached Palestine in 1881, just in time to help a newly arrived group of destitute Yemenite Jews who were being ostracized by some local rabbis who didn't consider them Jewish enough.

Eight years later, Horatio Spafford died of malaria. And because the American consul froze the family's funds in a well-meaning effort to force them to go back home, the surviving Spaffords ended up almost as impoverished as the people they were trying to help.

But even then, Spafford House (as their mission/clinic was named) was a favorite stopover for the likes of British general Charles "Chinese" Gordon, who loved to spend hours with the Spaffords speculating on the probable location of Christ's crucifixion. Gordon's attention abruptly turned from Calvary to cavalry, however, when he was called away to put down a Dervish revolt in the Sudan. He was killed in the 1885 siege immortalized in the

Lake View

Charlton Heston movie *Khartoum*. To this day, the hill outside Spafford House—now a hotel—is called "Gordon's Golgotha."

In 1895, Anna Spafford returned home for a visit and brought back a group of Swedish Americans, many from Chicago, who set up a farm collective at least fourteen years before the first Jewish kibbutz.

By the time of the 1948 Arab-Israeli War, the mission was being run by the Spaffords' daughter, Bertha, who was unable to keep Palestinians from using the mission to fire on passing Israeli convoys yet wielded enough clout with both sides to at least arrange a two-hour cease fire when one of the clinic staff died.

Nearly twenty years later, Bertha's daughter, Anna Grace Spafford Lind, also had to learn diplomacy the hard way when an Arab demanded permission to use the clinic as an observation post. Realizing the Arab wasn't going to take no for an answer, Anna Lind reluctantly agreed only after he suggested dressing as a doctor to avoid drawing Israeli fire. When no surgeon's gown could be found, the equally reluctant officer ended up spying from the rooftop in a nurse's dress.

The center, still run by the Spafford family as a nondenominational medical mission, reportedly treats more than twenty thousand people a year, mostly children. In recent years, the clinic has run a special program for Arab, Christian and Jewish children suffering from the trauma of living in a war zone.

A more utopian religious vision swirled around the John McDonald House at 4211 North Hermitage, home to some of the North Side's poshest soirées in the early 1900s. There, in what was then one of the most fashionable parts of Ravenswood, Reverend George Hall and a handful of parishioners were planning a biblical exodus to an isolated religious colony in Florida. Hall, pastor of the Bush Temple at Chicago and Clark, actually managed to send forth a band of devotees to found a theocratic community just west of Florida's Lake Okeechobee. The Disciples of Christ colony lived on for years as Hall City before being absorbed by surrounding Glades County towns.

But in the end, Hall's main claim to fame turned out to be one of his sons, Wendall, who had started writing hymns at Bush Temple and eventually became a well-known radio singer. Dubbed the "Redheaded Music Maker," the younger Hall racked up several 1940s hits, including "It Ain't Gonna Rain No More."

After Reverend Hall's death in 1925, the house was bought by the evangelical Free Church, which ran a seminary there until after World War II. The three-story Queen Anne house was eventually razed to make way for an apartment building.

Rube Goldberg Would Have Loved These Guys Back in the Day

Lake View will never be remembered as the birthplace of the five-wheel automobile, the turboprop blimp or the conversion of coal into diamonds. Not that William Adams, Joseph Thompson or Frederick Schleeter didn't try back in the early 1900s.

Adams reportedly stripped down an Oldsmobile and installed a six-foot-wide wheel at the center, about where a modern car would have a transmission or drive shaft. The Roscoe Street resident hooked that oversized wheel to a two-cylinder engine and regularly tested his contraption along Marshfield Avenue between Lincoln and Addison, then one of the area's few paved streets. Although Adams tried to hold those shakedown runs in secrecy, his car was so noisy that it drew complaints from irate neighbors every time he got behind the wheel. To this day, nobody knows why both Adams and his contraption suddenly dropped out of sight forever sometime in 1902.

Thompson, on the other hand, did all he could to draw attention to the blimp he was building in his garage near Lincoln and Cornelia. A big sheet draped over the front door proclaimed "The Home of the Lake View Airship." But unlike most blimps, this one had a wind tunnel running right through the middle with a propeller at the very center, much like today's turbojets.

Thompson had hoped to compete for a $50,000 prize in the 1906 St. Louis World's Fair against Alberto Santos-Dumont, one of the world's leading lighter-than-air pioneers. To help meet expenses, Mrs. Thompson even started her own neighborhood laundry.

Unfortunately, one summer evening, Thompson lit a cigar too close to the airship's homemade gas generator, an old whiskey barrel containing a mixture of zinc and hydrochloric acid that he believed would produce the volatile hydrogen used in pre-*Hindenberg* airships. The would-be aviation pioneer got off with minor injuries, but according to some stories, Mrs. Thompson had to take in laundry for years to come.

Not far away, on Henderson near Ashland, Fred Schleeter quit his diamond cutter's job to work full time on backyard experiments he just knew would lead to the conversion of coal into diamonds. Schleeter supposedly got the idea after hearing a high school physics teacher talking in a bar about how diamonds are nothing more than pure carbon crystallized under incredible pressure. Man-made diamonds eventually were produced from carbon, but not by Schleeter, whose wife also reportedly slaved away her sunset years over other people's laundry.

Lake View

But gullibility has apparently never been a rare commodity here on the North Side. During World War II, self-comissioned "General" Matthew Skarbeck of 2222 North Sacramento signed up three thousand mostly wealthy, attractive women for his Military Order of Guards, which the FBI at one point thought might have been a neo-Nazi front. A mounted unit led by "Major" Helga Smith of 1032 North Dearborn met three times a week at a riding academy at 2223 North Cleveland.

After Pearl Harbor, hundreds lined up to enlist in what they thought was an officially sanctioned Home Guard unit. Later, one especially patriotic lassie marched down to the Oak Street beach and peeled off her army-type uniform, revealing a scanty swimsuit, in an apparent attempt to stimulate recruiting.

By the end of 1941, the Illinois National Guard's adjutant general had sent the outfit a letter ordering a stop to what he called the "promiscuous" use of the uniform. Two years later, the order was still being ignored, prompting the U.S. secretary of war himself to order state authorities to have the group disbanded, explaining that while there was no proof subversives had infiltrated the group, the potential was always there.

So on August 10, 1943, hundreds of Skarbeck's troopers dutifully assembled in the Cleveland Avenue stables to formally stand down. Seconds later, they turned around and took the oath of enlistment in Skarbeck's just-created Blue Dragoons and then went home to dye their uniforms and fade into oblivion.

COP SHOP, BALLPARK, CHA HOMES, THEATER PROVE REINCARNATION

The 1873 town hall at Addison and Halsted where Billy Boldenweck made his Alamo-like last stand seems to have always been a center for controversy. Even before it was built, local residents were complaining when the Lake View Village Board paid a seemingly exorbitant $2,900 for the corner property and then spent another $17,000 putting up a two-story, five-room building topped by a huge dome.

After the suburb was annexed by Chicago fifteen years later, the town hall was used for community meetings, theater performances and sometimes even church services (as well as a firehouse) in the early 1890s before it was recycled into a police station. The old landmark was finally replaced in

The Lake View House, built in 1853 at Byron Street and Sheridan Road, was a popular North Side hotel until around 1890.

1907 with the present building, which at least three times almost became a community center once again. That was one of the suggestions being considered in 1975, 1983 and 1987 when the city announced plans to close town hall and merge it with the 19th District on the old Riverview site at Belmont and Western.

As far back as 1966, the controversial police superintendent Orlando Wilson—who was never actually a policeman but a California law enforcement professor—came to Chicago. A special selection committee that he himself headed picked Wilson in the wake of the 1960 "Burglars in Blue" scandal that triggered what was until then the biggest shakeup in the department's history. "O.W.," as he was known, said a station as old as town hall couldn't "provide the space and modern equipment necessary for today's police needs."

While even a 1947 study complained about the small and dirty lockup, the century-old landmark has had its memorable moments—like in 1969, when a bomb went off just outside the building. Or when a college teacher came in to report the theft of his rooster. Or when a lady of the evening who was being booked at the front desk offered oral sex to a reporter if he'd post her bond.

Nevertheless, all good things must end, and in 2010, the old town hall station was replaced with a nearby $30 million, two-story, forty-four-thousand-square

Lake View

foot "police campus" able to accommodate 450 officers working three shifts, as well as a one-hundred-seat community meeting room, a gym, interrogation rooms, holding cells and a secure lineup room where crime victims and witnesses can safely identify suspects without themselves being seen.

City officials plan to renovate the 1907 building as part of a housing complex and community center for elderly gays. So the old town hall will live on after all as Lake View's most famous building next to Wrigley Field, which also has had nine lives, or so it would seem.

The latest chapter in the story of one of America's first housing developments was written in 2010, when the city announced plans to turn the Lathrop Homes at Diversey, Damen and the Chicago River into Chicago's first "green" public housing complex. While it's not clear what any new building would look like, developers would be required to meet gold or platinum LEED certification standards. "We're shooting for the stars here. We want the revitalization process to be one of the best. It has to be the standard-bearer," then–1st Ward alderman Manny Flores said. Planners want at least one-third of the units reserved for public housing families, with the rest of the nine hundred units offered as market rate or subsidized rents.

Dedicated by First Lady Eleanor Roosevelt in 1938, the Lathrop Homes had been the subject of heated debate and wild speculation since the 1990s, when rumors began circulating that the whole thirty-acre site, located as it was in the rapidly gentrifying Hamlin Park neighborhood, would be sold to a private upscale housing developer.

The original two-story houses and three- and four-story apartment buildings have been considered eligible for inclusion in the Illinois Register of Historic Places by the Illinois Historic Preservation Agency and the National Park Service since 1994. The complex has been on Landmark Illinois' list of the most endangered places in the state since 2007.

Affordable housing was just as much an issue when the Lathrop Homes were built as it is today, with the Chicago Housing Authority getting nine applications in 1937 for each of the original 925 available apartments. Early records show that most of the families moving into the Lathrop development had annual incomes of less than $1,500. Preservationists have been trying to keep Chicago's first public housing development from ending up as landfill.

Over nearly ninety years, the one-time theater building on the 1600 block of West Belmont has been dismissed as an eyesore and welcomed as a landmark in the making. Urban historians argued for the Belmont's preservation even as the terra cotta façade began crumbling, narrowly missing more than one passerby in the early 1980s.

Hidden History of Ravenswood and Lake View

Theater historians say the Belmont was possibly the North Side's most lavish vaudeville palace when it was built in 1926 by Baliban & Katz to compete with the Orpheum Circuit's Lincoln Hippodrome in the Wiebolt's building a few blocks away. Even after live shows were discontinued in favor of movies, the old theater was taken over periodically for community gatherings ranging from the seventy-fifth anniversary of Lake View's annexation by Chicago to Kiwanis Club minstrel shows and cooking classes sponsored by the Lerner neighborhood newspapers.

By the 1960s, the Belmont had become a bowling alley that was finally shut down after a November 1972 fire that left one woman dead. In 1981, the building was taken over by the Federal Savings and Loan Insurance Corp. and sold for an undisclosed sum to Ken Goldberg, a controversial developer who promptly announced plans to turn the place into a twenty-five-store shopping mall. When that scheme fell through, Goldberg put in a flea market, a low-end furniture store and a martial arts school—all the while talking about how he was "very close" to leasing the crumbling local landmark to an out-of-town cinema chain.

In 1986, a promoter even offered to lease the building for a laser war games center complete with carpeted tunnels, walkways, battlements and an observation deck. But again, nothing came of it.

Wrigley Field, the nation's second-oldest major-league ballpark, where the fans finally saw the lights on August 8, 1988. *Photo by Patrick Butler.*

Lake View

By early 1992, finding a new life for the Belmont Bowl—or razing the empty building—became one of the top priorities in local architect Dana Blay's master plan for revitalizing the flagging Lincoln-Belmont shopping district. "Actually, there aren't as many building violations as you might think," said Goldberg shortly after he took over the old theater/bowling alley. "The guys who designed and built it aren't around anymore. They don't know how to make buildings like this today."

By the mid-1990s, the old Belmont vaudeville house/movie theater/bowling alley had found new life as an upscale condo complex anchored by a beauty spa.

A few miles away, Wrigley Field—already among the country's oldest major-league ballparks and the lone holdout against night games—finally caved when organized baseball announced it wouldn't allow any postseason games there unless the lights went on in the otherwise Friendly Confines. It was a long time coming. In 1942, then-owner P.K. Wrigley was about to install lights but cancelled those plans because of World War II. It would be another forty years before the Cubs again talked about lights in Wrigley Field.

But the prospect of lights in Wrigley Field wasn't the first time the neighbors howled. Back in 1914, when restaurateur Charles Weeghman and his partners wanted to build a "ball yard" for their Chicago Whales baseball team at Clark and Addison, opponents warned it would only bring saloons, rowdy crowds and traffic problems. Neighbors pointed to a city ordinance requiring community approval of any major new project. Many of those residents had moved in when the Chicago Lutheran Seminary was still on that corner. But in 1910, after nearly twenty years, the Reverend William Passavant's divinity school moved on to the "healthier air" of suburban Maywood. Despite heated opposition, Weeghman and his partners got the one thousand signatures needed to build a ballpark on the site.

Zachary Taylor Davis, the same architect who had designed Comiskey Park four years earlier, built the new Whales Stadium with five hundred men in only five weeks at a cost of $250,000. But within two years, the Federal League folded. Weeghman and his nine partners, including chewing gum magnate William Wrigley, bought the Chicago Cubs and moved them from the West Side to the fourteen-thousand-seat ballpark. Once again, not everyone was pleased. Purists denounced the ivy foliage as a "desecration" of sorts.

Wrigley, who quickly became the majority owner, introduced reduced price "ladies' days" in 1919.

Between 1921 and 1970, it was also home to the National Football League's Chicago Bears and hosted the 2006 Gay Games and the second annual National Hockey League Winter Classic in 2009.

The Chicago Cubs' first at-home night game was held on August 8, 1988, despite years of community-instigated lawsuits and protests. Ironically, the game against the Philadelphia Phillies was called after only three and a half innings because of a rainstorm. Neighborhood residents saw the deluge as a message from above. "God is peeing on the Cubs," crowed Charlotte Newfeld, leader of the anti-lights Citizens United for Baseball in Sunshine (CUBS). The first complete night game at Wrigley was held the following evening, this time against the New York Mets.

The number of night games allowed at Cubs Park is still limited by an agreement with the Chicago City Council. And Cubs officials still meet routinely with the community to discuss mutual concerns.

Shortly after buying the Cubs franchise in 2010, in fact, Thomas Ricketts assured the neighbors they would be consulted more often before future decisions are made. "We're not a corporation anymore. It's a family. We're going to make decisions like a family," he told an audience that included three aldermen.

But even that wasn't good enough for residents like Sean Delanty, who wanted to know when the Cubs were going to win their first World Series in more than a century. If the Cubs were to go all the way in 2010, "there would be parties in Tibet," Delanty said.

Of course, anything can happen to a ball club that almost became known as the Trojans. During eighteen different (mostly sportswriter-inspired) name changes, the Cubs were at various times dubbed the Colts, Rainmakers, Rough Riders and Remnants. In fact, the Cubs were once known as the White Stockings long before the White Sox. After winning the National League's earliest pennants in 1876, 1880, 1881, 1882, 1885 and 1886, early sportswriters abbreviated the White Stockings to the Whites. In 1887, after a number of veteran players were replaced by rookies, the team was again rechristened the Colts, a nickname that was dropped the following year in favor of the Black Stockings following yet another uniform change.

By the turn of the century, Charles Comiskey had resurrected the name White Stockings (which he almost immediately shortened to White Sox) for the all-new major-league team he was putting together near the South Side stockyards. To confuse things even further, the one-time Colts became the Ex-Colts and later the Rainmakers (because of the number of times they were rained out during the 1898 season) before the sports reporters finally settled on yet another moniker, the Orphans.

Lake View

Later, when they began going to New Mexico for spring training, the Orphans were renamed the Cowboys and then the Desert Rangers. By 1901, their ranks again decimated by defections to the American League, the Orphans became the Remnants, who finished the season in sixth place with 53 wins and 86 losses.

The miserable showing led new manager Frank Sales to bring in still more new blood, prompting sports reporters to christen the club the Chicago Cubs. In 1905, after George Murphy bought the team, the Cubs briefly became the Spuds. By 1908, however, they were again the Cubs—this time with their own emblem, a large C enclosing a little bear holding a baseball bat.

The name finally seemed to be sticking after the team won three consecutive pennants and the 1907 and 1908 World Series. But then in 1913, second baseman Johnny Evers (originally from Troy, New York) became manager, inspiring some papers to call the Cubs the Trojans. Evers was canned after one season. Although he returned as manager eight years later, the Trojan nickname fortunately didn't.

1971 Indian "Uprising" Spreads from Ballpark to Missile Site

During the summer of 1971, Wrigley Field also became the unlikely protest site for a handful of Chicago's fourteen thousand American Indians who camped out in wigwams at the front gate to protest poor housing conditions.

While nobody ever explained what the ballpark had to do with Indian housing, most of the Indians quickly headed for the lakefront to seize a recently vacated Nike missile site in Belmont Harbor. At about the same time, an anxious nation was watching the standoff between Lakota Sioux protesters and FBI agents at the Wounded Knee, South Dakota reservation.

Inside the compound, Indian spokesmen like Mike Chosa vowed not to be intimidated by the dozens of police surrounding the abandoned army outpost.

"My heart leaps like an eagle," Chosa told a reporter as he watched the "bluecoats" moving into position, preparing to deal with what looked like Chicago's first Indian "uprising" in nearly 150 years. "Any day is a good day to die," said Chosa, who had obviously seen the movie *Little Big Man*, making the rounds at local theaters that summer.

But in early July, after a siege lasting several weeks, police and park workers routed some fifty Indians in a predawn raid censured that very evening by the

Lake View Citizens Council (LVCC). Neil Ganz, chairman of the LVCC's Nike Site Committee, said the forcible eviction solved none of the problems that led the Indians to take over the vacant army outpost in the first place.

Deputy Patrol Chief Robert Lynsky said police never intended to move out the Indians but only provide protection for work crews being brought in at 5:00 a.m. to tear down a seven-foot-high wire fence surrounding the vacant missile base. The plan changed when the Indians resisted with clubs, bricks, bottles and even firebombs, one of which destroyed a $10,000 sailboat anchored in the harbor.

Despite the LVCC's censure, the Indians' action drew sharp censure even from Father Carl Lezak of St. Sebastian's Church, who after leaving the priesthood served briefly as Illinois director of the American Civil Liberties Union and the LVCC's executive director.

Archbishop Sheil Got Boys Boxing, Battled Bigotry and Fear

It was no wonder the park field house at 3505 North Southport was named for an archbishop who lived only a few blocks away at St. Andrew's Church at 3546 North Paulina. After all, Bernard Sheil wasn't your typical priest.

Fresh out of seminary just before U.S. entry into World War I, he found himself serving as chaplain at the Cook County Jail, where he almost fell through a gallows trapdoor trying to stay as close as possible to one of his "parishioners" who was about to be hanged. During his fifty-nine years as a priest (thirty-one of them as pastor of St. Andrew's) and forty-one as an auxiliary bishop, Sheil always took that extra step.

A star pitcher at St. Viator's Seminary in Kankakee who played for the Logan Squares baseball team during his summer vacations, Sheil turned down contract offers from both the Chicago White Sox and the Cincinnati Reds so he could be ordained on schedule in 1916.

After service as a World War I navy chaplain at Great Lakes Training Center and his assignment at Cook County Jail, Sheil was made a monsignor for his success in organizing the 1926 Eucharistic Congress in Soldier Field, the first international church event of its kind ever held in the New World.

Four years later, he got Cardinal George Mundelein to let him set up the Catholic Youth Organization to help curb juvenile crime, if nothing else. "Of course, if a young man can get to see God in a pair of boxing gloves, so much the better," he mused. Cardinal Mundelein unwittingly ended up sponsoring the biggest boxing tournament ever held in Chicago: the Golden Gloves, still an annual event at the St. Andrew's Gym built by Sheil.

Over the next thirty-five years, Sheil expanded the CYO to include an airplane pilot training school at Lewis College in Lockport, Illinois; WFJL-FM radio; the country's first remedial reading program; and readjustment assistance for young Puerto Ricans and Japanese Americans. The "Apostle of Youth," as he was soon being called, managed to round up guide dogs for the blind and collect funds for Navajo Indians in Arizona.

The archbishop also became the first non-Jew ever given B'Nai B'rith's national humanitarian award and helped found the Lake View Council on Religious Action to promote ecumenicalism long before most North Siders had even heard the word. The council was also intended to counter the growing influence of Nazi Bunds and the Ku Klux Klan then making alarming inroads in Chicago. "The only Jew anyone need fear is the one in his own imagination," Sheil warned.

Early North Side Park Was Literally Scooped Out of Clay...

If there was any justice in the world, Hamlin Park probably would have been named for Albert Hahne instead of Abraham Lincoln's first vice president. After all, Hahne was the brick maker–turned-alderman who, in 1911, got the city to convert the one-time quarry at Wellington and Damen into one of the North Side's first public parks.

It also housed one of the North Side's first public libraries. Before then, the library system operated through a network of "delivery services," often in pharmacies or dime stores, where patrons went through lists of available books, turned in their requests to the druggist or cashier and then waited the few days it took for books to arrive by horse-drawn delivery wagons.

Old-timers recall that until it moved to 2205 West Belmont, the library was at least as popular as the swimming pool and athletic fields where A.C. Buehler of Victor Comptometer played football and future County Board president George Dunne and State Representative Charlie Fleck were early park supervisors.

Originally owned by Otto Zapel, the quarry had become a farm by the turn of the century when Thelma Hoffman used to take a cinder path to get to Schneider School, still at 2957 North Hoyne. "I used to be thrilled by a medicine show that set up business in a woody lot in back of the Galilee Baptist Church," Hoffman recalled years later in John Drury's *North Side Notebook* in the early 1950s.

"Halloween was always a festive time. They always had bonfires and passed out apples," recalled real estate salesman Jerome Levatino, whose brother Jim, longtime president of the Hamlin Park Association, ran the baseball league that attracted as many as eight hundred players every season.

Jerome Levatino, whose family lived in the neighborhood since the 1920s, said he "practically grew up in the park," which had a jogging track decades before running became the rage. It may also have been one of the first parks anywhere in the city to offer tennis, Levatino added.

…AND CLAY MADE LAKE VIEW CENTER OF U.S. TERRA COTTA INDUSTRY

A ready supply of clay also paved the way, so to speak, for Lake View's once-vibrant terra cotta industry. And while it's been more than half a century since the Northwestern Terra Cotta Company shut down its West Lake View works, much of the largely long-forgotten company's best advertising is still all around us.

There's the Wrigley Building on Michigan Avenue and the old Reebe Storage near Clark and Fullerton, built to look like an Egyptian temple during the hype following the discovery of King Tut's tomb back in the early 1920s. There's even the block-long Terra Cotta Place two blocks from the 1750 West Wrightwood plant where 2,700 employees toiled back in the days when Lake View was the center of America's glazed brick industry.

The Reimer-Kuenster Brick Co. had its quarry at Diversey and Ashland, just across the street from the mansion originally built in 1907 for the president of the Illinois Brick Company.

Not far away, Northwestern, one of the city's earliest factories and one of the few to survive the Chicago Fire, was getting its clay from a block-long pit at Ashland and Diversey and by the mid-1880s was turning out $300,000 worth of masonry a year. Later, Sanford Loring, the company's treasurer as well as a practicing architect, turned Northwestern from just another brick maker into one of the leading creators of ornamental materials.

Lake View

Most of the plant's supervisors lived along Clybourn, and many of the first pupils at Prescott School at Ashland and Wrightwood were children of Northwestern employees. A number of executives like John True (the city of Lake View's last treasurer before the suburb was annexed by Chicago) were so politically active that the company's main office on Clybourn became something of a city hall annex.

Adolph Hottinger, son of the plant's president, recalled in a 1930s interview how most turn-of-the-century employees walked to work because "the horsecar line from downtown came only as far as Clybourn and Ashland." But even the few with their own transportation weren't much better off, he added, because "Clybourn was often so muddy, buggies and wagons got stuck in the mire for hours."

One of Northwestern's first contracts was to supply bricks for the landmark Rookery. Its biggest job was the Wrigley Building at Michigan Avenue and the river. And for years one of Northwestern's most recognizable local projects was the Lake View Bank building at 3201 North Ashland.

That landmark façade came down during a 1957 renovation—at about the same time Northwestern Terra Cotta itself, which had never recovered from the Depression and the trend toward simpler building design, shut down its Chicago operations, closing its last plant, in Denver, Colorado, in 1965.

WHY SOME CARPENTERS, STABLE OWNERS SAW FUTURE IN NEXT WORLD

When some of Lake View's pioneer furniture makers and stable keepers wanted to put new life into their businesses, they knew where their best markets lay: in coffins, of course.

Back in the 1880s, funerals were just starting to come out of the family parlor into newfangled mortuaries. All you needed to break into the business was a hearse, some carpentry skills and maybe a correspondence course in embalming, which had been growing in popularity since the Civil War. For the first time, traveling undertakers worked the battlefields preparing the remains of well-heeled soldiers for shipment home at the families' expense.

Heinrich Birren, however, didn't have to wait for the war to see a future in the afterlife. The Luxembourg-born carpenter and blacksmith worked at the Cyrus McCormick reaper plant several years before opening his carriage repair shop. He became a funeral director in 1859 after being asked to build a fancy hearse for the city's only mortician at the time.

One of Birren's sons, Cornelius, eventually branched out with his own funeral home on North Avenue, while another son, Peter, opened Lake

Christian Krauspe, who opened this furniture store in 1887, converted it to a funeral parlor a few years later after seeing opportunities in the underground economy, so to speak.

Lake View

View's first mortuary in 1885 at 2927 North Lincoln Avenue. Another Birren funeral home opened at 6125 North Clark Street.

Christian Krauspe followed the Birrens into the business five years later after running a successful furniture shop at 1628 West Belmont in a two-story frame house he put up for $800. In 1892, Ernest Schmidt opened still another funeral parlor on Belmont near Western. And in 1897, the Burkhardt Mortuary opened in the family stables at 3847 North Lincoln Avenue.

By the early part of the twentieth century, of course, mortuary science was becoming a profession in its own right, requiring formal schooling and state licensing. And today's laws in most states, incidentally, prohibit the use of once-popular embalming chemicals like strychnine and mercury. It had become too hard to investigate suspected poisoning deaths.

"Yellow Kid" Weil Wished He'd Gone into Politics Instead of Jail

There was only one thing legendary con man Joseph "Yellow Kid" Weil considered impossible: "You can't cheat an honest man."

After forty-one arrests and ten years behind bars for swindles that reportedly netted him at least $10 million back in the days when that was real money, he ought to have known what he was talking about.

Credited with masterminding the first phone swindles and elaborate setups like hiring scores of actors and renting a ballroom that he sold to a man who thought he was buying a nightclub, Weil insisted his well-heeled victims had it coming.

"The upper crust is full of crumbs and they're the least likely to go to the police," Weil observed shortly before his death at age one hundred in a Sheridan Road nursing home. "How would it look for a banker to complain he'd lost $57,000 on a device to duplicate money?" Weil wondered.

He drew the line, however, at going after women's assets "because they'll either squawk or fall in love with you and take up the time you should be spending working on others."

Still, even the Kid wasn't above having a little fun now and then—like the time he tried to sell a horse and some goldfish to bailiffs while he was waiting to be locked up for a racetrack con job.

He and his trademark John Philip Sousa beard and pince-nez glasses had in fact become so notorious that lookalike U.S. senator (and erstwhile presidential hopeful) Hamilton Lewis begged him to shave his whiskers. At one point, even his lawyer, Clarence Darrow, advised him to "just get out of town."

After one last stretch in Joliet Penitentiary, the Kid announced his "retirement," claiming he'd lost his touch. He moved into an apartment at 420 West Melrose, tried his hand at charity fundraising and then wrote his autobiography and a pamphlet on effective sales techniques.

Going straight never proved profitable. Weil and some of his associates lost $375,000 on a circus they bought that was rained out for twenty-two days straight! In the end, the Kid was on public aid with less than $200 to his name but only one regret: that he didn't become a politician.

After all, he said, "L.B.J. did the same thing I did, taking from the rich. The only difference is that he got to be president while I got five years."

Swedish Roots Still Run Deep Enough for Two Visits by King

When King Carl XVI Gustav visited Chicago for the second time in April 1988, he spent most of his time at the new Swedish-American Museum at 5211 North Clark and other Andersonville highlights. It was the second time in only about two years that the Scandinavian monarch toured what was once the world's second-largest Swedish city.

By then, there was practically nothing left of Lake View's much-older Swedish community on the 900 block of West Belmont. All that remains today is Ann Sather's Restaurant—and that's owned by an Irishman, 44th Ward alderman Tom Tunney.

The Old Orphei Singing Club at Irving and Ashland is now the Jose Rizal Center, serving the much newer Filipino community, and the Svithoid Society has moved from the 600 block of Wrightwood to Portage Park on the Northwest Side.

The one-time Cooperative Temperance Café at 3206 North Wilton Avenue has been recycled more times than anyone can remember. And the old Salvation Army Swedish Corps once located a few doors north disbanded in the face of rampant gentrification.

Unless someone told you, you'd have no way of knowing that the 3200 block of North Wilton was once the home of Lake View's first Swedish settler, John Enander, and for years was a center of Midwest Scandinavian life. It was there

Lake View

that the poet, historian, orator and educator who had once been introduced to future president William McKinley as a "household word" among America's Swedes wrote his seven books, including a two-volume history of the United States that was translated into several languages during his lifetime.

The future Republican power broker and newspaper editor walked off the boat in 1869 with only twenty cents in his pocket and not knowing a word of English. Enander nevertheless managed to get into Augustana College in Rock Island and in 1876 moved to Lake View, where he built his Wilton Avenue home seven years later.

Except for three years teaching Swedish language and literature at his alma mater, which issued him an honorary doctor of laws degree in 1893, Enander was editor of the Swedish-language newspaper *Hemlander* until his death in 1910 at age sixty-eight. He was eventually showered with honors, including a decoration from Sweden's King Oscar for both his literary output and his political and civic work in his new country.

Enander served for a time on the Illinois State Board of Education, started both the Swedish-American Historical Society and the Westgoth Association, organized a campaign to get a statue honoring Swedish botanist Cark Linnaeus in Lincoln Park and helped found Trinity Lutheran Church at 1218 West Addison. His service as a speaker at the Republican National Convention and his success as a whistle-stop campaigner for President Benjamin Harrison got him appointed U.S. minister to Denmark in 1889.

Enander's widow, Malinda, lived in the Wilton Avenue house until 1918, when it was taken over by the Salvation Army's Swedish Corps. The now almost-forgotten agency eventually became the Salvationists' Lake View Corps, which merged in 1980 with a neighboring congregation at 1415 West Belmont. By then, the Lake View Corps' registered membership had dwindled to fifty, with only twenty still active. Most of the Swedes had moved up to Andersonville in their third great migration since settling around North and Wells in the mid-nineteenth century.

Just who gave Andersonville its name probably depends on whether you're talking to a Scotsman, a Norwegian or a Swede. Back in the 1950s, *North Side Notebook* author John Drury credited Scottish stonecutter James Anderson with giving the community its name. Anderson, Drury said, was born in Scotland in 1841 and came here twenty-three years later to carve tombstones at Rosehill Cemetery. He eventually became postmaster of the Roes Hill suburb and was succeeded by Hattie Anderson, who may or may not have been a relative.

Hidden History of Ravenswood and Lake View

That was the wrong Anderson, said Odd Lovell, another writer who insisted that the area was really named for a Norwegian Lutheran pastor, Reverend Paul Anderson, who lived there in the 1880s before moving to Colorado for his health. Lovell, a Norwegian who taught at St. Olaf's College in Minnesota, argued that people didn't used to pay as much attention to the way they spelled names as they do now.

"Ridiculous," snorted the late Richard Bjorklund, a one-time president of the Ravenswood–Lake View Historical Association who just happened to be a Swede. Bjorklund noted that Norwegians usually end their names with "*sen*," while Swedes—like Scots—prefer "son," conceding that the two longtime rivals made an even bigger deal about it in years past than they do now.

Reverend Andersen, Bjorklund said, "was a wholly estimable man" who started an English-language Sunday school and even held Swedish services in his Near North Side church, but "there's no way he could have founded Andersonville," Bjorklund said. After all, the Scotsman James Anderson was barely a toddler and Pastor Paul Anderson hadn't even started at Beloit College back in the 1840s when a Swede named John Anderson bought a farm just north of what would someday become Clark and Foster, the center of today's Andersonville.

At least part of the property was soon sold to a German named Michael Weber and eventually used for the Andersonville School, where sixty-five voters took part in Ridgeville Township's first election in 1857. That "Little Red Schoolhouse" remained a local landmark until 1908, when it was replaced by Trumbull School at 1600 West Foster. The area would eventually be known as Edgewater (after an early subdivision) until the late 1950s, when Clark Street businessman Grant Johnson suggested reviving the name Andersonville as a way of remembering the neighborhood's Swedish roots.

Those roots grew so strong that by about 1910, Chicago's Andersonville was the world's second-largest Swedish city, right after Stockholm. While most of those Swedes' grandchildren have long since moved on, at least some of the old ways continue today. At 10:30 a.m. every Saturday, a bell ringer followed by a group dressed in Viking and Swedish folk costumes parade up and down Clark Street. As the bell ringer passes each store or restaurant, workers emerge with brooms and sweep the sidewalks in front of their businesses.

Most of today's Andersonvillagers have no idea how lucky they are to live there. Back around the late nineteenth century, another early developer named Zero Marx started a subdivision of his own between Balmoral, Foster, Clark and Glenwood. He wanted to call it Zero Park.

Lake View

"Children's Poet" Eugene Field Gone but Never Forgotten

Although he probably would have winced at the thought, Lake View had its own unofficial poet laureate in the person of Eugene Field, who, unlike most bards, was neither poor nor unknown while he was still alive.

He apparently also had what the Irish call "second sight." In early November 1895, as he was packing for a lecture trip to Kansas City, the already world-renowned literary lion mused to nobody in particular that "this is the dying time of the year." The next morning, the forty-five-year-old author of "Wynken, Blynken and Nod," considered by some critics the best children's poem ever written in the English language, was found dead of an apparent heart attack by his thirteen-year-old son, Fred (nicknamed "Daisy"), at what is now 4240 North Clarendon Avenue.

Word of his death spread instantly. Crowds flocked to the Sabine Farm, which is what Field called his rambling white mansion in then-suburban-like Buena Park bounded by Graceland Cemetery, Irving Park and Lake Shore Drive.

Broadway (formerly Evanston Avenue) looking north in the late nineteenth century.

His passing brought tributes from admirers across the globe, ranging from fellow poet Joel Chandler Harris to a crippled boy who showed up at Field's home asking for a farewell look at the "Children's Poet" whose "Sharps and Flats" in the *Chicago Record* had also helped establish the personal opinion column as a mainstay of modern newspapers.

Field had served his apprenticeship as a reporter and editor in St. Louis, Kansas City and Denver after bumming around Europe squandering an inheritance mostly on curios, including a robe he'd bought from a Japanese Buddhist monk just so he'd presumably be the only one in America to have one. But he had an uncanny way of replenishing his cash reserves. He even turned a profit on one of his hobbies with "Affairs of a Bibliomaniac," a humorous dissertation on his adventures in book collecting. He collected his front porch thoughts in his 1892 *Echoes of Sabine Farm* when he wasn't collaborating with his brother Roswell on a rhymed translation of the works of the Roman poet Horace.

While few topics were off-limits to the iconoclastic Field, his favorites seem to have been the pretensions of Chicago's meat barons (which he put in a book, *Culture's Garlands*) and unreliable public transportation ("The Oldest Horse in Chicago Works for the Lake View Street Car Company and Was Present at the Battle of Marathon in 490 B.C.").

Despite a rewarding career poking fun at pomp and privilege, even the Union League Club sent a wreath to his standing-room-only funeral at Fourth Presbyterian Church, where the hymns included "Singing in God's Acre," written by Field himself, and longtime friend Frank Gunsaslus delivered the eulogy entirely in verse. Mourners ranged from *Chicago Daily News* publisher Victor Lawson to Alcott School classmates of Field's two sons. Floral pieces included a broken pen, drum and trumpet commemorating what many consider Field's second-best poem, "Little Boy Blue," and a single flower that was all one little factory urchin could afford.

Not surprisingly, Field was soon honored with both a school (at 7019 North Ashland) and a monument built in 1922 just east of the Lincoln Park Zoo's Small Animal House. Years later, city architect Ira Bach called that memorial unique in that "it doesn't scare children like most statues do."

Eugene Field would have liked that.

Part II
Ravenswood

Is Ravenswood a State of Mind or a Real Neighborhood?

Just to the northwest of Lake View, Ravenswood's boundaries depend on whether you ask the city, the Ravenswood Chamber of Commerce or the Ravenswood Community Council. Each has its own boundaries. And on some maps, Ravenswood is more a geographical expression covering the North Center/Lincoln Square/Albany Park areas, also claimed by some to be separate communities.

Although touted as a tony refuge from the noise, smells and soot of the city, the area had far earthier beginnings than the Ravenswood Land Company would have wanted to admit when it bought 194 acres of farm and wooded land eight miles north of what were then the Chicago city limits, which is why it was years before Ravenswood got sewers. The developers wouldn't spend the money, forcing property owners to pay out of their own pockets. And even then, Jefferson Township wouldn't let Ravenswood's sewers run through its land to the Chicago River. It wasn't until 1889, when Lake View and Jefferson townships were formally annexed, that everybody got sewers.

As for the elegant Sunnyside Inn on Clark near Montrose, where both Abraham Lincoln and Stephen Douglas supposedly stayed, it didn't start out that way. Long before anyone called them "gentlemen's clubs," places like the Sunnyside Inn were offering sybaritic delights under direction of

Ravenswood

"Gentle Annie" Stafford, one of Chicago's most colorful madams, who'd often strike up conversations by asking patrons, "Who's your favorite poet? Mine's Byron."

The tone had been set back in the early 1850s when "Gentle Annie," so called because of the way she used a whip to propose to husband Cap Hyman, celebrated both her wedding and the hotel's grand opening with a nightlong bash described by one paper as "the swellest show" Chicago had ever seen. Guest of honor was Deputy Police Chief Jack Nelson, who according to one account was "by no means there in his capacity as a keeper of the peace." Most of the downtown gaming dens and bordellos closed for the night as revelers headed north for the party. Some, like a contingent from the Board of Trade, first met at the Matteson house at Randolph and Dearborn before boarding a gondola-shaped sled around 8:00 p.m. to the accompaniment of trumpet fanfares.

Fredrick Francis Cook recalled in his *Bygone Days in Chicago* that while the guests "without exception forgot to bring their wives, there was no scarcity of ladies." Indeed, every man was assigned an otherwise unoccupied trollop—and a cautionary by Cap Hyman that "this affair will be straight to the wink of an eyelash.

"All the ladies here are on their honor and Mrs. Hyman will see to it that nothing unseemly takes place. We want the best people in town to patronize Sunnyside."

Although several women were clearly impatient for "that honor thing" to be over, all went well until a midnight dinner brawl erupted after one indignant hussy felt her character was being impugned. By the time it was all over, a bystander recalled, "Ellen McMasters was constrained to wear her eyes in mourning for the rest of the evening. Another had her face left a mass of dissolving views, the red, white and blue each striving to be the dominant color." A third woman was reported to have "had her nose changed from pug to Roman. How much hair was bestrewed on the floor and what became of the waterfalls of hoop skirts in the conflict will never be known," Cook said.

But the troubles didn't end with daylight. "For many days after the event, police justices worked overtime issuing warrants for assault and battery," according to Cook. Among others who "completely lost their heads were Billy Bolshaw of the Matteson House. When I came on him a few days later, he showed me a wine bill for $500 and asked what I thought of it."

Previous, top: Lincoln and Montrose Avenues about 1910.

Previous, bottom: The Sunnyside Inn at Montrose and Clark Streets started in 1859 as a "high toned" bordello/gambling casino run by three-hundred-pound "Gentle Annie" Stafford.

Hidden History of Ravenswood and Lake View

Some neighbors, of course, weren't unhappy when Annie and her husband retired a few years later. And the Sunnyside eventually became the meeting place of the Ravenswood Land Company, developers of the suburb just north of what was then Lake View village. Some thought that was as respectable as it got. Then, in 1870, the Shadyside Inn—another infamous brothel "Gentle Annie" would have loved—opened just across the street.

Just how Ravenswood got its name has been open to debate for at least a century. One theory is that it was named for the Potawatomi Indian Chief Raven (or was it Black Partridge?) who lived in the woods along the Chicago River and allied himself with the first white settlers against the rival Mingo tribe. Or maybe it was the area's once-plentiful ravens.

But today's historians think the most likely possibility is that the name came from one of the Ravenswood Land Company's board members who hailed from a New England town of that same name. At least that's what the daughter of Martin Van Allen, the "Father of Ravenswood," always believed. Van Allen, one of the speculators who bought 194 acres along the Northwestern Railroad right of way, built the tract's first house at 4506 North Winchester Avenue. That house was razed in 1970 to make way for a Ravenswood Hospital expansion project.

By the early 1870s, Ravenswood was being touted as one of Chicago's most "aristocratic" suburbs, attracting mostly residents of "native American stock"

The first mail carriers at the Ravenswood post office, circa 1894.

Ravenswood

(U.S.-born white Protestants) like Samuel Godkins, who built a house that still stands at 4646 North Hermitage Avenue, which Carl Sandburg and his family called their "really, truly home" when they lived there in 1913–14. It was enough time to transform Sandburg from an unknown thirty-five-year-old sometime newspaper reporter into a nationally famous poet. It was there that he wrote his first book, *Chicago Poems*, published in 1915 with some of his best-known works, including "City of the Big Shoulders," and part of his second volume, *Cornhuskers*, which came out three years later. But contrary to local legend, his monumental biography of Abraham Lincoln that made Carl Sandburg a household word was done only after he'd moved to the suburbs.

Sandburg, incidentally, wasn't the first notable to live at the 4646 North Hermitage address. Godkins himself was a prominent lawyer who came here from Vermont by way of Indiana, where he'd briefly served as a judge shortly before the Civil War. His son, James Godkins, was a noted artist, one of the founders of the old Chicago Academy of Design and an organizer of the 1893 World's Fair.

James Godkins's fondest dream was to replace the city's streetcars with a subway, a fantasy almost realized by his son, a city engineer who in 1907 nearly sold investors like Philip Armour on the concept of underground transit. Unfortunately, the deal fell through at the last minute, and it would be another thirty years before Chicago finally got its subway.

Soon after the turn of the century, the old house on Hermitage was sold to Harry Moniger, who lived on the first floor and rented the upstairs. Sandburg moved there in 1913 after leaving Milwaukee, where he'd been secretary to Socialist mayor Emil Seidel, to become associate editor of *Systems* magazine. But he soon quit the business management trade journal to join the experimental *Day Book* newspaper, which tried to survive without any kind of advertising. To nobody's surprise, the tabloid folded, and Sandburg went on to the *Chicago Daily News*.

Although he'd left Ravenswood by 1916, his continued links with the neighborhood reportedly included occasional attendance at All Saints Episcopal Church and friendships with local figures like *Booster* newspapers founder Leo Lerner. Sandburg, in fact, visited Lerner almost every time he was in town for conversations that reportedly ranged from politics to hemorrhoids. "Anything that gave people a pain in the tail was fair game," an admirer recalled years later.

Although Ravenswood became part of the city of Lake View (which in turn was annexed by Chicago in 1889) in 1887, the tony atmosphere lingered for years afterward. According to an 1898 history of the area,

Carl Sandburg called the apartment on the second floor at 4646 North Hermitage their "really, truly home," where he and his family lived from 1913 to 1914. *Photo by Patrick Butler.*

Lake View Post Office staff, late 1800s.

Ravenswood

"Ravenswood proper is a prohibition district, no saloons being there except outside the borders of said district...the prevailing tone is one of conservatism and refinement."

All that exclusivity, however, evidently began eroding with the advent of public transportation. As early as 1874, Ravenswood was linked to downtown Chicago by fourteen trains a day, each used by an average of seventy-five commuters. Two streetcar lines were introduced in the 1880s, and Clark Street and Irving Park Road got their first electric trolleys by 1896. By 1905, the Northwestern Elevated Railroad Company extended what is now the Brown (Ravenswood) CTA route from Lincoln and Paulina to Western and Lawrence.

Unsung Civil War Hero May Have Helped Save Chicago

Should the Lincoln administration have given the "Father of Ravenswood," Martin Van Allen, a medal for helping to thwart a Confederate plot to seize Chicago during the Civil War? As local head of the Spartan Brotherhood, a semi-secret patriotic organization formed to fight subversion and sabotage here on the homefront, the one-time Illinois Central Railroad construction engineer probably deserves at least some credit for saving our city, if not our country.

Van Allen and his fellow Spartans probably did more than their share in keeping Southern sympathizers (known as Copperheads), antiwar activists and out-and-out enemy agents from freeing several thousand Rebel prisoners at Camp Douglas near 35th and Cottage Grove at the height of the 1864 Democratic National Convention. The Rebels' plan was to hold several dozen of the city's leaders for ransom before moving on to Rock Island, where hundreds of Confederate officers were being held, and then attack Union forces from the rear, cutting off supply

Ravenswood Land Company founder and behind-the-scenes Civil War hero Martin Van Allen.

lines and thus prolonging the war by at least a year. Actually, the plotters never figured on things going that far since the Democrats were expected to nominate "peace" candidate General George McClellan, who would immediately sign an armistice with Richmond after taking Abraham Lincoln's place in the White House.

And Mayor Richard J. Daley thought he had problems during the 1968 Democratic convention!

Fortunately, a network of informants, possibly including Van Allen, enabled authorities to squelch the plot just before street rioting orchestrated by Confederate provocateurs was to signal the start of the prison break.

At war's end, Van Allen and nineteen other members of the Ravenswood Land Company bought nearly two hundred acres of Lake View township land just west of the Chicago and Northwestern Railroad tracks. Van Allen bought the subdivision's first home, where the Ravenswood Methodist Church held its first services, led by Malcolm McDowell, whose daughter, Mary, later became one of the city's first social workers.

Within a year, Van Allen was elected to the Lake View School Board and became town assessor in 1870. By 1874, his house and grounds were said to be worth a then-hefty $24,000. He kept making improvements until 1890, around the time his son Frank left home to become a medical missionary and eventually founded one of India's largest hospitals. Another of Van Allen's children, daughter Jennie, became a noted composer in Los Angeles.

After Van Allen's death in 1903, the house was sold to a family named Phelps, then to a Mrs. Ida Bloemer and finally to Ravenswood Hospital.

The Van Allen family papers were given to the Ravenswood–Lake View Historical Society for safekeeping some years ago, apparently after all references to the Spartan Brotherhood and its activities had been expunged.

For Last Trooper, Living Poor Here Was Worse than Indian Wars

At the time of his death at age 101 in June 1973, Fred Fraske was officially listed as the last surviving trooper from the Indian Wars.

His biggest battle, however, wasn't in the wilds of Idaho, where he served in 1894, but trying to live on a $135-a-month veteran's pension with his daughter, Lilian, in their apartment at 3740 North Spaulding. In fact, the only time Private Fraske ever came close to real combat during his three years as a stretcher-bearer with the Seventeenth Infantry was when his outfit was sent to put down a small uprising that he recalled years later "ended before it really got started."

"We were prepared. That's the whole thing in a nutshell," Fraske explained several years before his death. "The chief explained to his braves there wasn't much they could do against 400 soldiers. So they drifted back to the reservation."

"Actually, the Indians weren't bad eggs, but they'd been abused," he added. "Aside from the times when they'd go into Cheyenne and shoot the lights out, we never had any serious trouble with them."

Fraske, who'd come to the United States from Germany with his family in 1877, said he joined the army mainly to help his widowed mother, who received most of his nine-dollars-a-month pay.

After his discharge, he returned to Chicago, where he worked as a house painter until his "retirement" at sixty-five and then spent another twenty-two years as a plant guard.

The ailing Fraske became a cause célèbre about a year before his death when his daughter went public with complaints about the Veterans Administration's "callous" disregard for the plight of old soldiers like her father who refused to either die or fade away. The VA responded by raising his monthly benefits from $130 to $160, prompting Miss Fraske to write then-president Richard Nixon asking how he'd like to try living on what amounted to about $40 a week.

North Center Was Once Just That—The Center of the North Side

Named because it happened to be in the approximate center of the city's North Side, North Center was given its name by local printer Henry Moberg. On October 21, 1921, at the urging of Moberg, the Lincoln-Irving-Robey Businessmen's Association (ancestor of the North Center Chamber of Commerce) officially named the commercial district from North End to North Center.

North Center has been home to Chicago's oldest radio station, possibly the city's longest row of car dealerships, America's first movie capital and probably our town's first anti-pollution crusade.

Back in the late 1860s and early 1870s, the one-time Ravenswood Land Company subdivision began getting $200 to $2,500 per lot in the area between Montrose, Diversey, Ravenswood and the Chicago River.

Above: The heart of North Center—the Lincoln-Damen-Irving Park intersection—about 1910.

Left: This #15 double-decker bus ran along Wilson Avenue and Sheridan Road to the Loop during the late 1920s. Modernized double-decker buses were a fixture on Sheridan Road up to the early 1950s.

Ravenswood

Besides the Indians, the first residents were workers in "Bricktown"—the riverside quarries that were eventually forced to move farther north when neighbors started complaining about smoke and fumes—paving the way, so to speak, for a shopping center at Robey and Graceland (Irving and Damen) and a nearby residential development by Charles Ford, who named Berenice, Grace and Fay (now Larchmont) Streets after his three daughters.

Because the former clay pits quickly became dumping grounds for garbage, housing developers steered clear, leaving the virtually abandoned properties for parks and the Mid-City Golf Course at Addison and Western, where they later built Lane Tech High School.

Not far away, in 1903, the Schuetzen Sharpshooters' Park was installing a "Figure Eight" ride considered the forerunner of today's roller coaster—and the beginnings of Riverview, which would one day advertise itself as "the World's Largest Amusement Park."

BACK IN THE DAY, RAVENSWOOD—NOT LA—WAS FOR STAR-GAZING

For the first two decades of the twentieth century, the Essenay Studios dominated the movie industry in Uptown, while stars like Tom Mix, Gloria Swanson and even Charlie Chaplin worked at the Selig Polyscope Studio near Oakley and Irving. When "Colonel" William Selig was unable to get Theodore Roosevelt to let him go along on a 1909 safari because the former president had given that job to a crew from the Smithsonian Institution, Selig found a T.R. lookalike, bought a worn-out lion for $400 and dressed some blacks from the South Side in loincloths as members of the "hunting party." Some scenes for *Big Game Hunting in Africa* were shot along the Chicago River, as was the lion, which was killed on the third try by a sharpshooter hired for the occasion. According to Adam Selzer in his book *Chicago Unbelievable*, the lion had never been in a real jungle. The safari's set was created in a sixty-by twenty-foot cage on Selig's outdoor lot near the river and Irving Park. "We've come as near to doing the real thing here as it can be done. Get ready for the hunt," Selzer quotes Selig as telling reporters during the shoot.

The film was finished just as the real T.R. shot a lion while on the safari Selig had hoped to cover. While the former president was never mentioned by name either in the film or the promotions, Roosevelt was furious but powerless to stop the release of Selig's film. Rumor has it the Medal of

Honor–winning hero of San Juan Hill was also annoyed at learning that Selig was only a self-appointed colonel.

By 1911, the Selig lot had twelve lions, nine lion cubs, an elephant, ten leopards, seven leopard cubs, five pumas, a monkey, three bears, two deer, ten Eskimo dogs, eight gray wolves and an assortment of horses, mules, dogs, chickens and ducks. Selig found himself out of business within five years after following filmdom's exodus to California because Chicago's harsh winters didn't lend themselves to year-round shooting. Industry historians say Selig Polyscope Studio went belly-up partly because of the 1914 recession and partly because he apparently never realized "shorts" were about to be elbowed out by feature-length movies like D.W. Griffith's *Birth of a Nation*.

"There will always be the 'little pictures,' just like there'll always be vaudeville."

All that remains of the Selig empire today is the diamond "S" logo over one of the doors to his former studio (now a condo building) on the 3900 block of North Clarendon.

Faith Can Move Mountains—and Even Our Lady of Lourdes

In late 1928, Ravenswood was the site of one of the great engineering feats of the early twentieth century—thanks to the ingenuity of a local priest.

When the city told Father James Scanlon that Our Lady of Lourdes Church stood in the way of plans to widen Ashland Avenue, he literally decided to turn things around to his advantage. Instead of letting them chop 10 feet off the front, he decided to move the ten-thousand-ton church across the street and turn it halfway around so it faced north on Leland. Scanlon then cut the 100- by 175-foot building down the middle and inserted a 20-foot addition, increasing the seating capacity from 800 to 1,370.

Engineers and architects from around the world came to watch as a handpicked crew of 150 men slowly lifted the building off its foundations on 2,500 jacks and then edged it across the street on four thousand rollers after using air drills to clear away several inches of ice still coating the street that

Opposite, top: In what was considered one of the most remarkable engineering feats of the era, Our Lady of Lourdes Church was cut in half and moved across Ashland Avenue when the city widened the street in 1929. *Photo by Patrick Butler.*

Opposite, bottom: The Wright house at Montrose and Greenview, early 1900s.

Ravenswood

frosty March. To keep from pulling too hard on one part of the building, six heavy chains in front and six in the rear were hooked to seventy-two pulleys connected to four horse-powered capstans. On a signal from a whistle, the teams turned the capstans and the church began to move about a foot a minute, stopping every four feet to check lines and replace rollers as needed.

Crowe Brothers, one of the Midwest's oldest building movers, had to post a $300,000 bond to cover any possible damage. But the calculations were so good that the building didn't suffer a single crack as it was being hauled across the street and then split down the middle for the twenty-foot insert and attached to a new rectory.

By the time the move was completed in May, Scanlon had a collection of newspaper clippings on the feat from all over the world.

Except in his own native Ireland. "Sure, t'was no news in Ireland," Scanlon reportedly growled years later. "They do things like that every day over there."

Abe Saperstein Began His Globetrotting Career at Welles Park

Abe Saperstein traveled more than five million miles to eighty-seven countries during his forty years at the helm of the Harlem Globetrotters. But he never really left the old neighborhood. The undisputed clown prince of basketball was still living at 2948 West Eastwood when his heart gave out in Weiss Hospital on March 16, 1966.

Born in 1903 in London's Whitechapel district (where Jack the Ripper cut a swath of his own less than fifteen years earlier), Abe Saperstein was four when his tailor father took the family to Ravenswood. Young Abe shot squirrels along the river near Lawrence Avenue and inevitably made a name for himself as the only Jewish athlete in his new Irish/German neighborhood. He played second base for a Catholic parochial school even though he himself want to a nearby public school, and when the time came, he went out for track, basketball and baseball at Lake View High.

Saperstein was too small to make the University of Illinois basketball team but was coaching at both Welles Park and nearby Queen of Angels grade school in 1925 when someone offered him $250 a month to manage the Savoy Big Five hoops squad sponsored by Chicago's biggest black American Legion post. By 1927, he had his men playing for pay, crisscrossing the Midwest in an old jalopy driven by Saperstein, who often filled in on the court himself and got the squad doing comic routines mainly to save their feet from the nightly pounding on makeshift gym floors. Once they even strutted their stuff in a hayloft.

Once, some twenty-five thousand spectators filled a bull ring in Madrid at 11:30 p.m. to watch the Trotters. And just before the 1948 Olympics, Soviet basketball players stalked his team all over Europe hoping to pick up some pointers. By the time he was through, there were three Harlem Globetrotter squads girdling the globe, often at the request of the U.S. State Department, which considered the team among America's most effective goodwill ambassadors.

During a visit to Melbourne, Australia, the Trotters outdrew the Davis Cup tennis matches. And five years before his death, Saperstein's boys played thirty games almost nonstop during a tour of Finland, Poland, Hungary and Romania.

Probably the only time Abe Saperstein ever failed at anything was in 1961, when his American Basketball League folded after just one season, a setback he once estimated lost him several million dollars.

Saperstein, who often said he—as a Jew—had a lot in common with blacks because "we've both been persecuted peoples," not only developed his own basketball greats like Goose Tatum, Meadowlark Lemon and Sweetwater Clifton but also urged friends in professional baseball to give a shot at the majors to Satchel Paige and Minnie Minoso, among others.

Still, Saperstein wasn't your usual crusader, insisting to the very end that he saw his Globetrotters "primarily as an opportunity to provide some badly needed laughs in this pretty tough world."

It came as no surprise when the Chicago Park District named the Welles Park Gym in Abe Saperstein's honor.

Famed Architect Louis Sullivan Wrapped Up His Career Here

Ravenswood was where you could say one of Chicago's most famous architects ended his career.

Even before it was finished in 1922, some of Louis Sullivan's critics compared the Krause Music Store at 4611 North Lincoln to a mausoleum. Which is especially ironic since within a few years, owner William Krause had committed suicide upstairs and Sullivan died a penniless alcoholic

The Krause Music Store, the last building designed by Louis Sullivan, has over the years been a funeral home, art gallery and studio. *Photo by Patrick Butler.*

in a South Side flophouse. Then, in 1929, the building was converted into a mortuary, although Krause's widow continued to own it until 1958.

The once-lionized creator of the Auditorium, the Carson Pirie Scott building and the old Stock Exchange ended up a usually unemployed anachronism with his insistence on elaborate ornamentation in an era of increasingly simple design. By 1934, Sullivan had drunk himself to death, embittered at being "ignored." He is buried in Graceland Cemetery, not far from the Martin Ryerson and Henry Getty tombs he'd designed in happier times.

"Tastes were starting to change, but he wouldn't change his ideas with them," architecture curator Wim deWit recalled at the opening of a 1986 Sullivan exhibit at the Chicago History Museum. "You could call it stubbornness or consistency to one's philosophical beliefs.

"In the end, it all depends on your point of view."

Abbott's First Lab Was Run Out of Town by Irate Neighbors

One of the country's biggest pharmaceutical companies got its start in a cramped Ravenswood apartment in 1888 because its founder, Dr. Wallace Abbott, got fed up with the substandard nostrums of the era and moved his operations to the suburbs at least partly because of all the noxious fumes and

Ravenswood

Right: The Wallace Abbott Mansion still stands at Wilson and Hermitage. *Photo by Patrick Butler*.

Below: Firemen from throughout the city battle a November 9, 1905 blaze at Dr. Wallace Abbott's newly acquired Tangwell Printing Plant, 4739 North Ravenswood. Abbott gave his contractor six months to rebuild—a deadline met by drafting virtually every idle worker in the saloons along Lincoln Avenue.

wastes emanating from his plant. While here in Ravenswood, his lab workers had to be sent home more than once after being overcome by fumes. And a November 9, 1905 fire destroyed the 4739 North Ravenswood printing plant he had bought to produce his mail-order catalogues and promotional materials. Fire department officials said a shift in the wind could easily have engulfed Abbott's pharmaceutical labs as well.

Abbott gave his contractor six months to rebuild, a deadline reportedly met by drafting virtually every idle worker in the saloons along Lincoln Avenue. By year's end, Abbott's profits came to $200,000, the exact loss of the fire.

The 150 pharmaceuticals Abbott promoted in his fourteen-page catalogue included Granular Effervescent Seiditz Salt, which the brochure promised "freshens and purifies the blood, the source of all health." By 1894, Abbott was even editing his own medical journal, the *Alkaloidal Clinic*, suggesting remedies for the grippe, diphtheria, scurvy, constipation, carbuncles and other ailments of the period. He attacked tobacco long before it became fashionable, calling smokers "unstable, to say the least, if not actually dishonest."

By 1914, when medicines such as aspirin became scarce because of World War I, Abbott offered Barbital. Novocaine likewise became procaine. One

Wolcott and Sunnyside, site of old Cubley home, late 1800s.

of Abbott's biggest sellers was Chlorazene, an antiseptic developed by a British doctor that helped save hundreds, if not thousands, of lives.

Earlier, Dr. Abbott, who gave a gold watch at Christmas to any employee who quit smoking, had been forced out of his original basement plant near Wilson and Ravenswood because of neighbors' complaints.

By the time Abbott died in the airy mansion that still stands at 1733 West Wilson, on July 4, 1921, at age sixty-three, the company was already moving again, this time to a twenty-six-acre site in North Chicago, where his workers continued research on synthetic medicines started during World War I and eventually turned out such products as Murine eye drops and Selsun dandruff rinse.

Shortly before his death, his trust foundation donated $50,000 to Ravenswood Hospital, which at one time had loaned him some basement space for a research laboratory. That foundation also built Northwestern University's Abbott Hall.

Abbott's seven-bedroom mansion later became a funeral parlor and the Khamis family homestead before it was recently bought by Abbott Labs for use as a pharmaceutical museum. That project was eventually put on indefinite hold.

47TH WARD WAS SCENE OF A GENERATION-LONG "DUEL OF THE TITANS"

For more than a third of a century, Ravenswood was home to two political legends: Ed Kelly, father of the "Fighting 47th," once considered one of Chicago's most efficient Democratic political machines; and the equally legendary John Hoellen Jr., who continued a Republican dynasty as Kelly hammered out the archetypical Democratic stronghold against all odds.

Ironically, Kelly, who often insisted he never wanted to go into politics in the first place, said he was on his way to Milwaukee, where he had been offered the presidency of the just-created Milwaukee Bucks NBA franchise in 1968, when the first Mayor Richard Daley asked him to take over a floundering 47th Ward organization with only about a dozen captains trying to handle eighty-five precincts and virtually no funds. Daley told Kelly he'd have to recruit his own precinct captains and raise most of the ward organization's operating funds himself. Undeterred, Kelly called in favors all over the city and quickly created what became the textbook example of an urban political "machine" in the best sense of the word. Ironically, he also ended one of the longest, most storied political reigns in Chicago history not with a bang but a whimper.

In November 2003, the seventy-five-year-old political kingmaker announced he would not be seeking another term as ward committeeman, emphatically denying rumors that age, ill health or fears that he would not be able to beat back a challenge by the ward's alderman, Eugene Schulter, had anything to do with his decision.

The nature of the unpaid job had changed dramatically since he took over the then-struggling ward organization at the request of Mayor Daley, who was also Cook County Democratic Party chairman.

Kelly said he planned to bequeath what he described as a "thankless job" to Schulter at the end of the current committeeman term. "I gave him a career. He was like a son to me," Kelly said, recalling how he got his one-time protégé his first public job as a janitor at Welles Park and later found a spot for him at the Cook County assessor's office.

Later, Kelly said, it was he who got Schulter slated for alderman. "And this is how he thanks me," Kelly told a reporter.

Far from holding Schulter back from even higher office, Kelly said he even wanted to get Schulter nominated for the 5th District congressional seat "if he had really been serious about running. Unfortunately, he [Schulter] only had two fundraisers, then dropped the idea," Kelly recalled, adding that over the years, "he seemed to have wanted to go his own way."

Looking back on a storied career he never planned on having, Kelly listed his biggest achievements as coming into the ward in 1968 to build a powerhouse organization with only eight Democratic captains to handle eighty-five precincts; helping to get the Sulzer Regional Library and the McFetridge Sports Complex built; building a new Welles Park field house; and removing the old Ravenswood YMCA, which he described as "an eyesore." Kelly also pointed with pride to his work with seniors and youth, as well as the Ed Kelly Sports Program, which "covered the waterfront."

And as for his one-time protégé, Eugene Schulter, Kelly said that despite their three-decade age difference, "I can still beat him [Schulter] one-on-one [on] the basketball court. Anytime."

While Ed Kelly said he planned to continue helping out at the ward office and remain "as politically active as I've ever been," helping out as a "coach" rather than a ward boss, he has gradually distanced himself from day-to-day politics, preferring instead to concentrate on his sports programs and fundraising for causes like Maryville Academy, one of the state's largest child-care facilities. "Now I'm running like a one-eyed dog in a meat market," he said shortly after stepping down as committeeman.

Ravenswood

Although Hoellen's father, John Sr., was GOP committeeman and the ward's alderman from 1926 to 1935, the young heir's succession was hardly guaranteed. The younger John Hoellen's political career, in fact, almost ended before it started. The day he filed for alderman, someone shot him outside his house. The returning World War II naval officer escaped serious injury only because the assailant's shotgun misfired and the pellets failed to penetrate the thick sheaf of publicity photos and news releases in Hoellen's overcoat pocket.

While the case against the shooter—a known hoodlum—was quickly dismissed, it inspired Hoellen to begin campaigning for a mobile crime lab, which eventually became a reality. The fledgling alderman also co-sponsored the first uniform allowance for police officers, and in 1974, he proposed creation of a 911 emergency phone service.

Hoellen also had a well-known love for arts and entertainment. In 1967, he proposed turning Meigs Field into a Great America–type facility to replace the just-closed Riverview amusement park. That same year, the art critic in him surfaced when he proposed a city council resolution to "deport" the just unveiled Picasso statue in Daley Plaza and replace it with a statue of "Mr. Cub," Ernie Banks. "If you want to get a piece of junk [in the plaza] just get two junk automobiles that had been in a collision on the Kennedy Expressway. They'll get attention and have a powerful story to tell," Hoellen said.

But during his seven aldermanic terms from 1947 to 1975, his greatest emphasis was as a zoning watchdog and providing basic city services, like getting a swimming pool built at Welles Park in the heart of his 47th Ward. "He was very much a neighborhood guy," said the late neighborhood newspaper editor and local historian Richard Bjorklund.

While the "machine" Democrats liked to portray Hoellen as a political gadfly, "he was in many ways a man ahead of his time," Bjorklund said.

And probably the main reason he got into politics in the first place was to settle a score with the Democratic organization, which he believed destroyed his father's political career and probably killed him. John Hoellen Sr. suffered a stroke after losing his reelection bid and died of a heart attack after an attempt to regain the seat. "My father was a casualty of the political process in Chicago. And that's the reason I have such a hatred for this political system," he told a *Chicago Tribune* reporter shortly after retiring.

During his twenty-nine years as alderman, John Hoellen Jr. battled waste, gangsters and city hall corruption. Once, when Hoellen pointed out that far too many city "engineers" didn't have the requisite licenses, the powers that be responded by getting the state Civil Service Commission to repeal the state license requirement.

Not that Hoellen was surprised. After all, for years he was such an outsider that he didn't even have an office in city hall, despite his being a duly elected alderman.

But even that kind of humiliation didn't keep Hoellen from running for Congress three times—or twice running against Richard J. Daley, first for county clerk in 1954 and then for mayor in 1975. In the end, he even lost his aldermanic seat to a twenty-seven-year-old Eugene Schulter while he was concentrating on unseating Mayor Daley.

He would later attribute his defeats at least partly to a reluctance to ask people for campaign money. "I guess I wasn't a very good Republican," he laughed.

After ending his twenty-nine-year city council career, Hoellen was appointed to the Chicago Transit Authority (CTA) board by Republican Illinois governor James Thompson. During his decade and a half on that board, Hoellen not only rode the Ravenswood line nearly every day to the CTA offices at the Merchandise Mart but was also the only board member to become a qualified CTA bus driver. "He went through the training program so he'd know firsthand the kinds of problems the drivers faced," Bjorklund said. And while he was at it, Hoellen proposed a fare-card system much like the one we have today.

He also practiced law for more than fifty years in a family-owned building at 1940 West Irving Park and founded the Bank of Ravenswood to provide a ready lending source to local business and industry.

Hoellen also helped organize the Ravenswood Conservation Council (precursor of the Ravenswood Community Council) in the early 1960s, became active in the old Ravenswood YMCA and served as president and general counsel of the Germania Club. "He liked to be a force for good," Hoellen's widow, Mary Jane, said at his funeral. "His attitude was to get up and fight again when you lose in politics. You just don't lie down."

Which might have been still another reason why the ward was called the "Fighting 47th."

"Inebriated, Opium-Eating Women" Helped at Washington Clinic

When Illinois' first clinic for alcoholic- and drug-addicted ladies opened at Irving and Western in 1882, it created quite a stir. After all, those were the high Victorian years in more ways than one. And "nice people didn't admit the problem existed."

Ravenswood

But by then, the Washington Home for the Cure of Inebriates already had a long trailblazing tradition. The Cook County Good Templars had discreetly opened the first Washington treatment center in a rented Near North Side house back in 1863. The twenty-three patients admitted that year included two clergymen, a cabinetmaker, a surgeon, a newspaper editor and a couple lawyers. Founding board members included Charles Hull, whose home at Halsted and Polk would eventually be taken over by Jane Addams for America's first settlement house.

By 1867, the home was the only facility in the entire state where courts could legally sentence drunks for treatment. The Chicago City Council even voted to give the clinic 10 percent of all saloon license revenues. Later, an annual lump sum of $20,000 was awarded instead.

In the early 1880s, the Washingtonian Society—which until then had treated only men—paid $15,000 to obtain the ten-acre Northwestern Military Academy campus for "the care, cure and reclamation of inebriated and opium-eating women." Treatment took from two to four months (compared to two to four weeks for men) and cost from five to fifteen dollars a week, with free care for the "deserving poor."

By 1900, 1,300 women and 26,000 men had gone through the Washington program, with perhaps 20 percent pronounced "completely reformed" at the end of treatment. Then as now, substance abuse treatment programs never claimed complete cures but merely tried to "drive out the effects [of drugs and liquor] from the system, build up the vitality of the patient, and restore him to a condition in which he is better able to resist temptation."

A 1915 annual report blithely noted that fewer drug-related cases were turning up, "probably because of the new law restricting the sale of morphine and cocaine," which until then could be bought without a prescription at any pharmacy.

By 1917, twenty-four states had already banned liquor sales, and a Washington Home report predicted that the nationwide prohibition everyone expected "will put us out of business." The next year, hospital officials attributed an already drastic admissions drop not only to "the growth of temperance" but also to World War I enlistments, a severe worldwide influenza epidemic and "the higher cost of alcohol." Convinced that all addiction treatment programs faced a "doubtful future," the Washington Home began turning itself into a general hospital in the mid-1920s.

By 1982, a century after moving into North Center, Martha Washington Hospital still had a ninety-bed substance abuse unit where patients of both sexes stayed an average of twenty-one days, with another twelve weeks in outpatient early recovery support groups. Several years later, services were expanded to include the city's first cocaine withdrawal program.

By the time the hospital celebrated its 125th anniversary, clinic officials didn't even want to think about a bicentennial, again hoping to have worked themselves out of a job by then. While that didn't happen, the hospital closed in the 1990s, and the site was sold to several market-rate and subsidized housing developers.

Sweet Smell of Success Lingers On at Buffalo, Horner Parks

It's no accident that North Side gardeners used to get their most fertile soil from the old Buffalo Park at Manor, Sunnyside and California. Even though the old Diamond Race Track burned down in 1900, the ground still had a certain—ahem—richness as late as World War I.

Started in 1883 by Jack Diamond, owner of a livery stable on the southeast corner of Leland and Ravenswood (then Commercial) Avenue, the trotting track covered the area between what is now Whipple, Montrose, California and Eastwood. According to the late local historian Richard Bjorklund, Diamond's racecourse catered to trotters owned by Marshall Field and Cyrus McCormick (who used to test his reapers on a 480-acre Albany Park spread owned by gentleman farmer/diplomat Richard Rusk, who also had his own track at Albany and Lawrence).

Eventually, the Diamond racetrack boasted a grandstand and stables at Montrose and Richmond. By then, however, the ponies were getting so much competition from bicycles that clubs like the Ravenswood Wheelmen started meeting regularly at Diamond's track.

Eventually, Diamond either sold the business or took on partners. By the late 1890s, the course was listed on tax rolls as being owned by the Ravenswood Racing Association.

Diamond, however, evidently retained his sense of civic duty to the very end. In his history of Ravenswood Manor, Bjorklund points out how on every election day, the track owner would give local residents free rides from his livery stable to the old Lake View Town Hall (now the 19th District Police Station at 850 West Addison).

If it weren't for the garbage, the one-time brickyard at California and Montrose might have been the University of Illinois–Chicago campus instead of Horner

Ravenswood

Ravenswood Wheelman's Club members, shown here in front of their clubhouse at Wilson and Ravenswood around the turn of the century, when cycling clubs were all the rage. By the end of the nineteenth century, more than fifty clubs had a total of at least 100,000 members—enough clout to press the city council and Illinois legislature for bicycle-friendly legislation and smoother streets. Carter Harrison II credited his 1897 mayoral victory to "wheelman" support he rewarded with a bicycle path along Sheridan Road from Edgewater to Evanston.

Park, which incidentally would have been Joseph Ross Park, in honor of a once-popular local politician, if several hundred neighbors had gotten their way.

Back in the mid-1950s, U of I officials were looking at several possible sites, including the old Bach Brick Yard, but settled on Harrison/Halsted after soil tests showed the buried, decaying garbage couldn't support the underground pylons needed as foundations for high-rise buildings.

The site became a dump in 1935 after Bach finally shut down after forty years under pressure from local residents fed up with pollution. While the Bachs, who still lived at Manor and Wilson, were hailed as "good people who sold well-baked bricks," the ash from the manufacture of those well-baked bricks eventually made it impossible to grow grass anywhere on the southeast side of Ravenswood Manor. Housewives complained that the air was so dirty their wash got dirty even before it was taken down from the backyard clotheslines.

After the Bachs sold to the city, the open quarries were filled in with an estimated 280,000 loads of garbage. Within a year, neighbors were again complaining, this time about the stench, mosquitoes, rodents and overall filth. While people living near the Stockyards on the South Side got used to the odor because it was always the same, the Ravenswood dump treated residents to new smells with each load of garbage, Bjorklund said in a pamphlet on the history of Ravenswood Manor that he wrote in the 1960s.

One neighbor sought advice from Joseph Ross, a doctor as well as 40th Ward alderman. "Do what I do. Close your window," Ross counseled.

Others packed up and sold their homes at a loss before the city stopped dumping in 1947 and sold the old brickyard, now the north half of Horner Park, to the Park District for $119,000. The fifty-five-acre park and field house were finally dedicated in 1957 after one last neighborhood campaign. Local residents wanted the park named for Ross, who had led the fight to have the dump converted to a park. But park and city honchos decided instead in favor of Henry Horner, a longtime judge who served as Illinois governor from 1933 to 1940.

But that wasn't the only time people had to press for a decent neighborhood park. For years, they called nearby Welles Park "Pussyfoot Park" for a variety of good reasons. Some said the nickname probably stemmed from official "pussyfooting" around a tangled web of titles and deeds that reportedly held up development of the park for years in the early 1900s. The eastern part of the park between Lincoln Avenue and what is now the field house wasn't even owned by the Park District but leased from the C.K.G. Billings estate. Neighbors complained that park district officials were just "pussyfooting" when it came to buying the land once and for all.

On the other hand, there wasn't much "pussyfooting" going on in the park itself, where Prohibition-era street gangs reportedly took over at night and an irascible farmer at Sunnyside and Western allegedly used to plow up the outfield of the main baseball diamond whenever he got drunk, which by all accounts was often. Nor was there any "pussyfooting" in 1957, when a coalition of more than thirty local groups, led by Republican alderman John Hoellen (47th Ward) and Democratic committeeman George Wells, bombarded park officials with petitions signed by five thousand local residents demanding a new field house to replace the "tinderbox" built in 1913 as a "temporary" facility.

It took more than ten years, but the community finally got its new field house, complete with a seventy-five- by forty-five-foot swimming pool, club rooms and a gymnasium that has since been named in honor of Harlem

Ravenswood

The band from the Fifth United Presbyterian Church, Wolcott and Leland Avenues, 1907.

Globetrotters founder Abe Saperstein, who got his start coaching at Wells while living in nearby Ravenswood Manor. Although Saperstein's protégés became world famous for their fancy footwork, nobody ever accused them of "pussyfooting."

CHANNEL HELPED CLEAN UP AFTER "EPIDEMIC" THAT NEVER HAPPENED

"The river stinks. The air stinks. People's clothing, permeated by the foul atmosphere stinks. No other word expresses it as well as 'stink.' A stench means something finite. Stink reaches the infinite and becomes sublime in the magnitude of odiousness," belched the *Chicago Times* in 1880.

Five years later, the situation had become so intolerable that the city created the Chicago Sanitary District, headed in the late 1890s by Billy Boldenweck, the same feisty Lake View mayor who refused to hand over the just-annexed suburb's funds or records until forced to do so by the Illinois Supreme Court.

Hidden History of Ravenswood and Lake View

Western and Leland, 1938.

To protect Chicago's drinking water, the Drainage Board, as it was originally known, decided to literally reverse the flow of the river with a $29 million Sanitary and Ship Canal hailed at the time as the greatest engineering feat ever attempted by a single city. An extension of that project was the North Branch Canal, built over three years at a cost of $428,000 to straighten 2.2 miles of the Chicago River from its meanderings through West Ravenswood Gardens just east of Manor Avenue. From May 10, 1904, through December 2, 1907, workers dredged a canal ninety feet wide and twelve feet deep from Belmont to Lawrence, putting in three temporary bridges later replaced by the city. Completion of the job not only meant the beginning of the end of typhoid fever on the North Side but also forever changed Ravenswood Manor's east boundary.

The North Branch project paved the way for creation of the North Shore Channel to Wilmette, finished in 1910. Before the channel, drainage often flooded much of the North Side from Montrose Avenue (where snakes lived under the sidewalks) to the farms as far north as Foster Avenue.

In his later years, F.G. Anderson, a longtime resident of 4532 North Francisco who grew up on a ten-acre farm at Montrose and St. Louis, liked to recall how he'd skate for several miles over frozen sewage overflow during one especially cold winter in the 1890s.

The Sanitary District (now called the Metropolitan Water Reclamation District) was created after an 1885 summer deluge backed up tons of sewage into the city's water supply, triggering a cholera epidemic that supposedly killed eighty thousand people, or one out of every eight Chicagoans. It's a gripping story, but it never happened.

While it's true that a major storm that summer dropped five and a half inches of water in eighteen hours, washing sewerage from the Chicago River out into the lake, a check of the records showed no more than one thousand typhoid deaths that year and no records of cholera epidemics since the 1860s.

What would have been one of the biggest public health disasters in American history may have been averted by a wind shift that pushed sewage farther out into the lake and away from the city's then woefully inadequate sanitary facilities, according to Cecil Adams of the *Chicago Reader* and Libby Hill's *The Chicago River: A Natural and Unnatural History*.

Nevertheless, the fable continued into the early twenty-first century, when even the venerable *Chicago Tribune* retracted stories it had run earlier about the so-called killer epidemic. Nobody, including Libby Hill, seems to have any idea how the urban legend got started. But it just won't go away.

Three Brothers Who Became Admirals Got Their Start Here

Abe Saperstein, of course, wasn't the only notable to come out of Ravenswood in the past century. Daniel, William and Philip Gallery may be the only three brothers in American history to end up as navy admirals. And if you count the time their brother Reverend John Ireland Gallery spent as a chaplain, the one-time Paulina Street residents have collectively given more than 125 years to the navy.

Best known of the brothers, of course, is Dan Gallery, who made history in 1944 when he captured *U-505* in the first high-seas boarding operation by an American crew in 132 years, despite warnings that the maneuver was "impossible." Dan Gallery, who died in 1977, was on the U.S. wrestling team in the 1920 Olympics, later organized the first Little League in Puerto Rico and wrote more than thirty novels, mostly about navy life. In 1968, the then-retired officer infuriated Pentagon hardliners after North Koreans seized the USS *Pueblo* and tortured crew members into signing bogus confessions by suggesting all U.S. servicemen be given blanket clearance to say anything necessary to get their captors to release them.

Far less controversial was brother William, who died in 1981 at age seventy-seven after years as executive director of the United Republican Club. William Gallery held weekly luncheons at the Chicago Press Club, where he often acted as an intermediary between feuding factions of both political parties. It wasn't the first time William Gallery had done the seemingly impossible. During the Korean War, he got the USS *Princeton* out of mothballs in six weeks instead of the more usual six months.

The third brother, Philip, who died in 1973 while golfing in Florida, became a leading World War II destroyer commander after earning the Legion of Merit for organizing antiaircraft defenses along the Virginia coast practically from scratch.

The family's real expert on miracles, however, was Father John, best known for his efforts to get Ireland's Matt Talbot canonized as the patron saint of alcoholics.

Army's Top Engineer Spent Decades Trying to Prove Innocence

If you want to find out about Captain Oberlin Carter, another Ravenswood military notable of a different sort, you'll probably have to go in person to the National Archives in Washington. The longtime Ravenswood resident accumulated yards of transcripts during the forty-one years he spent fighting his way through twenty-seven separate federal court decisions before Congress finally overturned his 1898 court-martial conviction for allegedly taking $2 million in kickbacks from contractors making harbor fortifications in Savannah, Georgia.

Carter, considered the army's top engineer soon after his 1880 graduation with the third-highest grades in West Point history (trailing behind only Robert E. Lee and Douglas MacArthur), had already moved on to a new assignment as military attaché at the American embassy in London when he was arrested. He insisted he was innocent and continued to do so even while serving his three-year sentence at Fort Leavenworth. Stories persist that President William McKinley agreed but was assassinated in 1901 before he could issue a pardon.

After his release, Carter moved to Chicago, where he became a consulting engineer and longtime president of the Ravenswood Manor Improvement Association. At his home at 2947 West Wilson, he would hold frequent patriotic poetry readings on the front lawn and mapped

Ravenswood

strategy for a continuing fight to clear his name that went all the way to the U.S. Supreme Court.

When he died at age eighty-eight in July 1944, Carter willed $18,000 of his $105,000 estate to his housekeeper and companion, Madge Dillon, thirty, of 4756 North Manor, with the rest of the assets going to various relatives. Captain Carter's lifelong struggle to vindicate himself, however, came with a heavy price, as his heirs soon discovered after his burial in Graceland Cemetery. Besides some real estate, including a 150-acre farm and the Wilson Avenue house, Carter was reportedly down to his last $1,200 in cash at the time of his death.

Forgotten Musical Star's Legacy Still Lives On at Local Library

A 1984 Ravenswood–Lake View Historical Association essay contest entry by Wally Stearns is probably all that's been written about Mattie Vickers Rogers in more than seventy years. Yet around the early 1900s, she was easily the sweetheart of America's musical comedy, starring everywhere from the Corn Palace in Mitchell, South Dakota, to the old Bugg Theater on Damen Avenue near Irving Park.

Her father was a retired actor who ran a boardinghouse, so it probably didn't surprise anyone when she made her own vaudeville debut in the mid-1870s at Colonel Wood's Museum in the Loop. Mattie Vickers not only stayed in the business, but in 1877, she married her manager, Charlie Rogers, who six years later even wrote a musical, *Jack*, for her to star in.

She eventually found her niche specializing in comedic German accent roles at a time when most other character actresses were busy parodying Irish brogues. According to one account, "No Corn Palace festival would be complete without the charming comedienne, Mattie Vickers, with her wooden shoes and her 'How you vas, anyhow?'"

After her husband's death in 1888, she traveled the country, starring first in *Circus Queen* and later *Edelweiss*. A book of Mattie Vickers songs from *Edelweiss* came out in 1891, around the same time the Mattie Vickers Comedy Company was offering free tickets to women accompanied by escorts with paid tickets.

By then, she'd more or less settled down in the Ravenswood area, becoming a regular at the Auditorium Theater while doing benefits like *Rip Van Winkle*

Mattie Vickers Rogers, a once-famous nineteenth-century actress whose diaries and memorabilia are part of the permanent North Side history collection at the Sulzer Library.

for the Ravenswood Hospital Aid Association.

During the summer of 1919, she gave one of her last performances, a recital at Ravenswood School. She also ran the Select School of Dancing and Elocution at Bennett Hall, 1776 West Wilson, offering ten lessons in "society" dancing for five dollars, with stunt training for ten dollars.

By the 1920s, Mattie Vickers had moved to 2217 West Giddings and finally to 2177 West Sunnyside in a two-story house still standing near the Sulzer Library, where her papers have become part of the neighborhood history collection.

Keeping Kids in School Was a Lifelong Battle for William Bodine

"One box of cigarettes and a five-cent novel like *Jack the Cop Killer* will make any boy a truant," warned William Bodine of 1225 West Sunnyside, who spent almost as much time campaigning against the tango as battling the turn-of-the-nineteenth-century's dropout rate.

Born in Missouri in 1862, Bodine (no relation to the Lake View–based electrical equipment company) came to Chicago nineteen years later and then moved west. There he became a newspaper reporter, Colorado state labor commissioner, vice-president of the National Association of Statisticians and special U.S. Court commissioner in Omaha, Nebraska. By 1895, he was back in Chicago as a political reporter for the *Times/Herald* and

Ravenswood

four years later was compulsory education superintendent at a time when absenteeism was rampant among the city's 255,000 schoolchildren.

He promptly organized a free bus service to take handicapped youngsters to classes; distributed lunch to an estimated five thousand needy pupils; and battled against child labor and neglectful parents. Over a six-year period, Bodine prosecuted more than two thousand truancy cases and, by 1902, had founded the first Chicago Parental School near Berwyn and St. Louis Avenues. There, chronic truants sentenced by the courts rose at 6:00 a.m. to the sound of a bugle, spent the day studying and doing military drills and finally turned in at 9:00 p.m. after Taps.

Civil libertarians like Clarence Darrow had fits. One school board member warned that the practice of training kids with wooden guns would only turn out a whole new crop of streetcar robbers. "I don't want to teach the young blackguards to shoot us," the board member yelled during a particularly heated meeting.

But Bodine argued (some of his foes would have thought appropriately enough) in *Big Brother* magazine that "the paternalism of the state becomes necessary when the paternalism of the home fails." The daily drills were only a form of disciplined exercise, countered Bodine, who was far more worried about the pernicious effects of modern dances like the tango ("It's wrestling," he said) and "society women" who set a bad example by smoking. "Cigarette smoking and the evil communion of the street accounts mainly for the lack of mental aptitude and school attendance in small boys," said Bodine in his 1906 commission report.

Bodine wasn't any more successful in his later effort to have all lead pencils used in the public schools sterilized as a precaution against mumps, scarlet fever and other childhood maladies.

Before his death at eighty-nine, Bodine also managed to write a book on child welfare and self-published booklets of poetry like *The City*

Two boys show off a snake in a park somewhere in Ravenswood during the 1890s.

Wonderful and *When the Irish Went to War*, in which he credits Hiberno-Americans with winning World War I.

He even found time to lock horns with "Bull Moose" Teddy Roosevelt, who considered the declining white birth rate "a form of race suicide." "Better race suicide than race decay," argued Bodine, who also believed the "New Woman" would dominate men and called Jews and Scots the ideal citizens because of their concern for education.

Curt Teich Brought the World Home with 265,000 Postcards

Where would you say some of the best postcard views of the Grand Canyon, the Eiffel Tower or the Rhineland were produced? In Ravenswood, of course. Chicago, in fact, was once the postcard capital of the world thanks to Curt Teich Company, whose plant at 1735 West Irving Park Road turned out 265,000 different designs between 1898 and 1976.

According to Katherine Hamilton-Smith, curator of the Curt Teich Postcard Archives at the Lake County Museum in far suburban Wauconda, "It was largely a case of his being in the right place at the right time." Picture postcards came into vogue during Chicago's 1893 World's Fair and soon became a favorite way to spread news of local happenings, according to Hamilton-Smith. "There were a lot of pictures of local earthquakes and other disasters that didn't make the papers in other parts of the country," she said, noting all that began to change in the mid-1920s when big newspapers started weekly rotogravure picture sections.

By then, Teich had become the world's biggest postcard printer, at one point employing more than one hundred artists to retouch photos taken by the plant's traveling salespeople across the United States and seventy-five foreign countries. The salespeople would take pictures of local landmarks or businesses and then try to get those businesses to order postcards to promote the local attractions, Hamilton-Smith said.

As a result, the collection includes scenes of once-popular local restaurants like Villa Sweden and the Brown Bear on Clark Street, as well as the Bankhead Tunnel in Mobile, Alabama, and Curt Teich's own hometown of Lobenstein, Germany. During the company's lifetime, the collection grew to include images of 100,000 towns and cities throughout the world and one of the largest collections of Route 66 and Lincoln Highway scenes.

Ravenswood

Other items still on film said a lot more than "Wish you were here" in an era when postcards—not bumper stickers or T-shirts—were used to spread a wide range of political messages. Those messages ranged from the "Faithful unto Death" Ku Klux Klan motto, complete with burning cross, to an early 1920s picture of an African American child proclaiming, "We're on the Rise."

Throughout the life of the company, until Curt Teich died in 1974 at age ninety-seven, the company saved fifteen copies of everything it ever printed. "They had so much space in the building they never really had to throw anything out," Hamilton-Smith said.

The old plant was converted in 1988 to the Postcard Place Lofts.

NORTH CENTER RADIO PIONEER TUNED OUT, BET ON LOCAL PAPER

More than half a century before Rupert Murdoch was forced by Federal Communications Commission regulations to choose between owning the *Chicago Sun-Times* or a local TV station, Clarence Wermich had to decide whether to sell the *North Center News* or WKBI, one of the area's first commercial radio stations.

Wermich's dilemma had nothing to do with the monopoly laws. And the 1929 Depression hadn't yet hit. Wermich, who'd been running both businesses almost single-handedly from his office on the fifth floor of what is now the MB Financial Bank at 3901 North Lincoln Avenue, just thought he was spreading himself too thin.

According to his daughter, LaVerne, who had served as a longtime board member of the Ravenswood–Lake View Historical Association, nobody who knew the broadcasting pioneer was surprised when he chose in favor of the paper that he ran until his death in 1965. "Newspapers," she said, "were his first love," even though Wermich had started the station first and turned publisher in the mid-1920s mainly at the behest of Alderman John Hoellen Sr., father of the longtime 47th Ward councilman, Republican committeeman and CTA board member.

A lifelong North Sider, Wermich attended Waller (now Lincoln Park) and Lane Tech High Schools, spent a year in DePaul Law School and even clerked for Henry Horner (who later became governor of Illinois and the namesake of Horner Park) before joining the navy and spending the rest of World War I at Great Lakes Naval Training Center. He returned home to take a job with A.W. Shaw Publishing, and shortly after the opening of WGN, now Chicago's oldest station, Wermich started WKBI, where programming ran from 1:00 to 9:00 p.m. weekdays (later on Fridays). Wermich ran almost continuous listenership surveys to find out whether audiences preferred more music, talk or political news.

Wermich soon found himself working virtually around the clock as announcer, ad salesman and station manager in a partnership with engineer Fred Schoenwolf that ended a few years after Wermich started the *North Center News* as a "sideline" in a second-floor office in the Hoellen building at 1940 West Irving Park.

According to LaVerne Wermich, WKBI was snapped up by WEDC, which at last report was still operating somewhere in the western suburbs.

Her father, who'd divested himself of the station to have more time to devote to the paper, was soon immersed in dozens of "outside" projects ranging from the Kiwanis Peanut Drive and the Neighborhood Boys' Club to the Billy Caldwell American Legion post. He was a founder of the North Center Commercial Association (forerunner of today's North Center Chamber of Commerce) and, during World War II, led campaigns to build memorials to local men killed in action overseas. Just days before his death in Augustana Hospital, Wermich was officiating at a North Center Lions Club meeting.

"Hero" Turned Out to Be the Killer in Sensational Mystery Here

Another Ravenswood resident and former army officer named Carl Wanderer almost got away with the perfect crime in which he killed his wife and unborn child, as well as the man everyone thought was the killer, until detective Sergeant John Norton and *Herald-Examiner* editor Walter Howey smelled a rat.

On June 21, 1920, Wanderer and his wife were returning home after seeing *The Sea Wolf* at the Pershing Theater at Western and Lincoln when a vagrant pulled a gun in the hallway of their apartment building at 4732 North Campbell Avenue. The ex-lieutenant and the assailant exchanged shots, and when it was all over, Ruth Wanderer and a man later identified as Al Watson lay critically wounded. Both died at Ravenswood Hospital a short time later.

To all appearances, it looked like Wanderer had avenged the deaths of his wife and unborn child by slaying the man everyone thought was their killer. He even had to be restrained from throwing himself on his wife's coffin during the graveside services. As far as most Chicagoans were concerned, Wanderer deserved a medal.

But when photos of the murder weapons, two identical Colt .45 automatics, began appearing on the front pages of the papers, Howey began wondering why a wino with only $3.80 in his pocket would have kept a gun he could easily have hocked at any pawnshop for an easy $10.00 or $20.00. Howey checked the serial numbers on the guns and discovered that although one of them was used at an army officer candidate school, the other had been bought in 1913 by a telephone repairman who said he later sold it to his brother-in-law, Fred Wanderer, who turned out to be Carl Wanderer's cousin. Fred Wanderer told police he had loaned the gun to his cousin the night of the murders.

Before long, police and reporters learned that far from being the victim, Carl Wanderer paid Watson ten dollars to stage a fake holdup, using a gun supplied by Wanderer, supposedly so the ex–war hero could impress his wife. But instead of chasing the "assailant" as planned, Wanderer shot Watson and Mrs. Wanderer in the darkened hallway. A search turned up pictures and letters linking Wanderer with a sixteen-year-old mistress. Police learned Wanderer was a swinger who had grown tired of his job at his father's butcher shop at 2711 North Western and wanted to rejoin the army.

In March 1921, Wanderer swung once more—this time from the gallows at the old county jail on Dearborn Street as he tried to sing the then-popular drinking song "Old Pal, Why Don't You Answer Me?"

Memories of Temperance Groups, Local Militias Still on Display

In the local history room of the Sulzer Library are a few mementos like the blue military cap used by a member of Ravenswood's own army and a small drum used by the Prohibition Drum Corps. The Civil War–style kepi was worn by a member of the Ravenswood Rifles, which gave exhibition drills every July 4, appeared at social affairs and offered its services at the time of the Pullman Strike and the Spanish-American War but was never called up. The weapons and uniforms had been provided by the National Guard at a time when a number of private militia units trained to serve as backup for the state troops if needed. One of the Ravenswood–Lake View Historical Association's first speakers was James McCurragh, who served as a sergeant in the forty-member outfit, which quietly disbanded in the early 1900s.

Hidden History of Ravenswood and Lake View

The Ravenswood Rifles in the mid-1890s was one of numerous private volunteer militia units organized by former members of the National Guard, which supplied the guns. The forty-man outfit drilled weekly, gave exhibition drills on national holidays and offered its services during the Spanish-American War and the Pullman Strike but was never called up. The Rifles also held socials at the Old Library Hall.

Ravenswood

The anti-saloon drum corps, which operated about the same time, would probably have been completely forgotten by now if Byron Jones, one of the corps' last surviving members, hadn't donated his drum to the local history society. According to Jones, the corps was the brainchild of outspoken prohibitionist Robert Greer, who had already helped organize a Ravenswood Woman's Christian Temperance Union chapter.

The band's twenty-one boys used to practice every week in a carpenter shop near the Northwestern Railroad tracks, recalled Jones, adding that members had to pledge abstinence from liquor, tobacco and profanity. Keeping members wasn't as hard as one might think, said Jones, noting that Edwin Cubley, who owned the factory that made the drums and other musical instruments, used to visit a local ice cream parlor every afternoon and buy sodas for "six or seven of the boys" who Jones recalled "thought the world of Mr. Cubley's drums."

RAVENSWOOD WOMEN'S CLUB WAS AS VICTORIAN AS IT COULD GET

When it finally disbanded in 1974, the eighty-five-year-old Ravenswood Women's Club was one of the oldest groups of its kind in Chicago. Maybe one of the reasons for its longevity was the practice of fining members one dollar for every uncompleted assignment. Delinquents also had their names posted on a bulletin board in their clubroom in the Paul Revere Masonic Lodge at Wilson and Ashland.

Founded by Mary Bassett in June 1889, the same month Lake View was annexed by Chicago, this club was made up entirely of well-off housewives who had all "acquired the dignity of a new baby and a hired girl."

Members had to respond at the roll calls starting each meeting with a famous quotation or pay a five-cent fine. When the ladies weren't listening to lectures on the "White Slave Traffic," "The Thoughtlessness of Today's Children" or "French History and the Life of Wycliffe," they debated whether couples should marry on $1,000 a year or less.

They also ran the lunch program at Lake View High School and made surgical dressings and furnished a room at Ravenswood Hospital. They even

Previous, bottom: The one-time Ravenswood Women's Club, later the Paul Revere Masonic Lodge, is now a Buddhist Temple. *Photo by Patrick Butler.*

helped found the Ravenswood Improvement Association partly to get paved streets for their part of the North Side.

During World War I, the club—the first to be chartered by the American Red Cross—knit socks and rolled bandages and later started collecting books to be sent downstate as traveling libraries. For more than seventy-five years, members made clothes for needy children. At one time, as many as five hundred dresses a year were sewn and distributed by club members.

But membership, which once topped three hundred, eroded as more and more women went off to work. In 1974, barely able to muster a quorum, the women disbanded, another casualty of changing times.

Today, the building is a Buddhist temple.

Was Bowmanville Named for Innkeeper Who Swindled Guests?

While many subdivisions were named after the developers' hometowns, wives or daughters, one—Bowmanville—commemorates one of the North Side's earliest real estate scams. Jesse Bowman sold an entire tract he didn't own and then vanished without a trace, forcing the purchasers to buy their property all over again. It's still uncertain whether Bowman deliberately defrauded these early settlers or just made an honest mistake—and whether any of the victims had anything to do with Bowman's disappearance.

But by the time the Bowmanville neighborhood officially became greater Lincoln Square, most of the disputed property had become part of the Budlong pickle empire. And this time there was no question about the title.

Once among the country's largest truck farms, the four-hundred-acre Budlong farms and pickle plant had two thousand workers, many of them railroad commuters from the Polish neighborhoods along Clybourn to Lincoln and Belmont, where they would be picked up by Budlong's wagons. The workers were originally paid at the end of the day in silver dollars, known as "Budlong Dollars" or simply "Budlongs."

The dynasty's founder, transplanted New England schoolteacher Lyman Budlong, started farming here in 1857 on land leased from an agent known only as "Mr. Foster" and opened his pickle factory twelve years later. In 1880, the Budlongs branched out into the flower business, and by the turn of the century, they had between eighteen and twenty greenhouses described by one visitor as "a virtual village of glass."

Ravenswood

Bowmanville's Budlong greenhouses, shown here in the early 1900s, were once among the nation's largest pickle producers.

Employees at the Budlong greenhouses.

The elder Budlong also found time to serve twenty-eight years as head of Jefferson Township's public schools and several terms on the Bowmanville village board of trustees. When he died in 1909, he was succeeded by his son Joseph, one of the founders of Lake View Bank and its president from 1913 to 1942. Joseph Budlong's son Thomas also became a Lake View Bank executive, while his other son Joseph Jr. headed the nearby Belmont Realty Company.

Although the Budlong Pickle Company disappeared in the 1960s and the last of the greenhouses were finally dismantled in 1988, reminders of the old days are still with us. The family name lives on in the Budlong Woods, once a game preserve where patriarch Lyman Budlong let his friends (and anyone else willing to pay a small fee) hunt raccoons. The tract later became a golf course from 1921 until the housing developers moved in.

Bowmanville is also remembered by a street running near Rosehill Cemetery, which some say would have been named Roe's Hill (in honor of Abram Roe, who ran a nearby tavern) if it weren't for a printer's error when the graveyard opened in 1859.

While it may not have the roster of socialites you'll find at Graceland, Rosehill has its own share of distinguished Chicagoans, among them thirteen mayors, including Buckner Morris, who was implicated in an 1864 attempt to help several thousand Confederate POWs escape from Camp Douglas and free the officers then being held in a camp at Rock Island. Together, the escaped Rebels were to attack Union forces from the rear. Morris, an outspoken antiwar Democrat married to a Southerner who often harbored escaped POWs in their home, was eventually acquitted. The other mayors include Daniel Boone's widely despised nephew, who provoked Chicago's first riot in 1855 when he tried to close the saloons on Sundays. Also buried in Rosehill is Civil War mayor "Long John" Wentworth, who wanted no inscription on his seventy-two-foot-high marker, hoping that people would be curious enough to go read about him.

From the world of arts and architecture are the graves of William Boyington, who designed Chicago's iconic water tower as well as Rosehill's fortress-like gate on Ravenswood Avenue; and Leonard Volk, who did the only life mask ever made of Abraham Lincoln.

Rosehill is also the resting place of 1920s "thrill killers" Nathan Leopold and Richard Loeb and their victim, Bobby Franks. "All I'll say is that they're buried within about 100 yards of each other," then–cemetery historian David Wendell told a reporter twenty years ago. Not far away are the graves of Al Capone hit man Frank Gusenberg and one of his victims, Dr. Reinhardt Schwimmer, an optometrist who was hanging out in the SMC Garage at 2122 North Clark the morning of the St. Valentine's Day Massacre.

Ravenswood

RAVENSWOOD RESIDENTS PLAYED OWN VERSION OF "NAME GAME"

Surprisingly, the Bowmanville subdivision's name wasn't changed until 1925, when it was rechristened Lincoln Square at a time when if you were looking for a name for a neighborhood, school, restaurant or athletic association, you couldn't go wrong to name it after Lincoln.

Until only a few years ago, a gas station at Grace and Wolcott was still called the Lincoln & Lincoln Garage because that's where it used to be located. From 1895 until 1937, Wolcott Avenue was Lincoln Street, one of five Chicago streets honoring the sixteenth president. Besides Lincoln Street, there were Lincoln Avenue, Lincoln Place, Lincoln Parkway and Lincoln Park West.

"The person living on the street will presumably be able to find his home, if he is temperate. But his friends and persons wanting to do business with him are likely to be confused," conceded Edward Brennan, who devised Chicago's street-numbering system in the early 1900s.

Edith Cubley of the drum-making family agreed. By 1935, she and her neighbors were insisting their street be changed back to its original name honoring Dr. Alexander Wolcott, an army surgeon and Indian agent at Fort Dearborn.

"Lawn mowers sharpened. Called for and delivered" promises a tradesman making his rounds along Western Avenue near Lawrence around 1920.

Mrs. Cubley and her neighbors weren't alone. The Ravenswood–Lake View Historical Association, Ravenswood Improvement Association and Ravenswood Women's Club were demanding name changes despite vehement opposition from at least one GOP alderman.

"If there were six Lincoln Streets, I couldn't ever vote to erase the name of a Republican saint from our city," he told the Lerner Newspapers in the late 1930s. "That would be partisan politics."

BIBLIOGRAPHY

Andreas, Alfred T. *History of Chicago*. Chicago: A.T. Andreas, 1885.

Encyclopedia of Chicago. Developed by the Newberry Library with the cooperation of the Chicago Historical Society. Chicago: Newberry Library, 2004.

Grossman, Ron. *Guide to Chicago Neighborhoods*. Chicago: New Century Publishers, 1981.

Hayner, Don, and Tom McNamee. *Streetwise Chicago*. Chicago: Loyola University Press, 1988.

Heise, Kenan, and Mark Frazel. *Hands on Chicago*. Chicago: Bonus Books, 1987.

Keating, Ann Durkin. *Chicago Neighborhoods and Suburbs: An Historical Guide*. Chicago: Bonus Books, 2008.

Lerner Newspapers, Chicago, 1965–1993.

Miller, Donald L. *City of the Century*. Chicago: Simon & Schuster, 2003.

Pacyga, Dominic A. *Chicago*. Chicago: University of Chicago Press, 2003.

Sawyer, June Skinner. *Chicago Portraits*. Chicago: Loyola University Press, 1991.

About the Author

Patrick Butler is a lifelong Chicagoan who has covered the North Side for the past thirty-five years, most of them as a reporter for the Lerner Newspapers. He currently writes for Inside Publications' *Booster* and *News-Star*. Butler served more than a dozen years as president of the Ravenswood–Lake View Historical Association and for several years anchored a cable TV news/feature magazine, *North Side Neighbors*.

www.ingramcontent.com/pod-product-compliance
Lightning Source LLC
Chambersburg PA
CBHW042144160426
43201CB00022B/2397